Fishing with My Uncles

Copyright © 2004
by William L. Robinson
Illustrations by William L. Robinson

First Printing 2004

Published by
Upper Peninsula Publishing
417 Summit Street
Marquette, MI 49855

Cover design by April Christian

All rights reserved. No part of this book may be reproduced or utilized in any form or by any means, electronic or mechanical, including photocopying, recording, or by an information storage or retrieval system, without permission in writing from the author. Inquiries should be addressed to:
William L. Robinson, 410 East Crescent Street, Marquette, MI 49855.

ISBN 0-9671-944-6-6
Printed in the United States of America

Fishing with My Uncles

by
William L. Robinson

Marquette, Michigan

Foreword

An original voice, at once hilarious and poignant, Bill Robinson shares with us a glimpse back to a simpler time. *Fishing with My Uncles* comes from the heart, as Robinson recounts adventures and fond remembrances of his years growing up in a close-knit family that honored the siren's call to outdoor adventure in the wilds of Michigan's Upper Peninsula. His keen memories will make you smile, sigh, laugh out loud and recollect similar adventures and people in your past.

As I read, I wished that I had been one of those who could tag along with the author and his uncles, as they acquainted him with the whims and virtues of the great outdoors, except, of course, the "almost" getting lost parts.

It's a wonderful, warm, funny read that puts us in pace with the roots of Bill Robinson, who grew to great stature as a highly respected wildlife biologist, professor, and lover of this great, wild land.

—Ann Wilson
Michigan Department of Natural Resources

Acknowledgments

I thank the following people:

My mother, Lucille Robinson, and my father, Thomas Robinson, for choosing to live in such a wonderful place as Marquette, Michigan, and its environs, and for taking me fishing, and teaching me how to catch fish—most of the time.

The many friends that I made because of a mutual interest in fishing, and the two families of Martin and Lowell Wilson, for taking me to good fishing places.

Richards' Sport Shop and the Schwenke Family for kindnesses and giving me flies at bargain prices, before I learned how to tie them.

The Parolinis, at whose camp we, as teenagers, often fished and stayed, enjoying the freedom of living without the supervision of parents.

My late uncles, Mutt and Loo, for putting up with me, when I must have been a pain in the rear end, and letting me catch fish that they, themselves, could have caught.

John Voelker, for taking the time to share his philosophies with me on a September day.

My late wife, Glenda, for tolerating my frequent absences from meals when the fish were biting, and serving as a wonderful friend and golf partner.

My daughter, Becky, who does not fish, but helped greatly in putting this book together.

And, lastly, my son, Tom, who catches more and bigger fish than I do, and does not rub it in.

Contents

Foreword v

Acknowledgments vii

Fishing in a Girl's Hat 1

Fishing With Uncle Tot 5

Catfish in the Bathtub—
Fishing With My Father 10

Fishing With Uncle Lockie 18

Just Loo and I 24

You Ain't No Six-Foot-One 29

The Knot 31

Mutt's Fly Rod 45

Embryology of a Fly Fisherman 48

The Quarry Pond 51

Hiking at Night in Underwear 59

Uncle Clarence, Frolings' Farm,
and the Wilsons 65

Religion and Trout Fishing 71

Fishing With Ernest Hemingway 73

A Trout Stream, A Man and Two Boys 80

Fishing with My Mother 84

The Summer of '51 88

Good Things Must End 92

The Disabled Veteran 95

Farewell to the Rebel 98

A Day with the Master 100

What It's All About 104

Last Day 108

Epilogue 113

About the Author 114

Fishing in a Girl's Hat

❧

My mother's family home faced the bay in Superior, Wisconsin. At a very early age, I learned that where there is water there are usually fish, and since before I can remember, I loved to fish. We had driven to northern Wisconsin from Iowa to visit my grandfather, aunt, and uncles when I was four years old. It was late May or early June, when much of the United States was enjoying spring. But Lake Superior generates its own weather, and when it comes ashore it is rarely good. The temperature was in the low 40s, and a cold drizzle was blowing in off the big lake, soaking and chilling anyone who dared to challenge it.

Fishing with My Uncles

I had been bored most of the day, sitting around the house listening to adults talking and laughing about things I did not understand. There were my Aunt Julia, my grandfather, my Uncle Lockie, and Uncle Tot. And here we were only yards from a great bay of Lake Superior, a virtual paradise, going to waste, in my opinion. I pictured fish swimming in the clear water, looking for food, maybe even waiting for me and my worms. In mid-afternoon I began a campaign of begging and pleading for my parents to take me fishing before the entire day was wasted.

But, as the afternoon wore on, I saw no effort to appease my longing to fish. I became less patient, and my parents found a new reason for me not to go fishing: I did not have a hat.

"I don't need a hat," I said.

"Yes you do," my mother insisted.

"Can't you find a hat?" I asked.

"Well, we can look for a hat, but if we don't find one, you can't go fishing. It's too wet and cold out there to go without something on your head," my father commanded. After a search of the entire house, my mother came down from the attic, triumphantly, carrying a woolen pink hood that had apparently been detached from a girl's jacket (probably my cousin Margaret's).

"Here," my mother said, "Put this on and we can go."

I looked at the pink hood. "I'm not going to wear

that," I said emphatically.

"Why not?" my mother asked.

"Because it's a girl's hat," I explained. "Everyone will think I'm a girl."

"Nobody knows you here," my mother reasoned, "It will keep your head warm and dry."

"I'm not going to wear it. It's a girl's hat," I said irascibly.

The next words were spoken loudly and clearly by my mother, with a space between each word. "If you want to go fishing you are going to wear this hat."

I put the hat on, grumbling. We dug a few worms from the garden, and my mother and father and I, carrying a Campbell's soup can with the worms, headed across the street with my steel telescopic fishing rod. We paused to let a car pass on the street, and I hid my face.

"That man thought I was a girl," I muttered.

Finally we began to fish, sitting on a plank that we turned over, and found to be relatively dry on one side. I was happy, and my parents at least tolerant, if not enthusiastic. I concentrated on watching the bobber, waiting for the tug of a perch or whatever might have been down there to take the worm, and only occasionally thinking about how stupid I must look in the pink hood. After perhaps a half-hour I got cold enough to quit, and did so without getting a bite, and without further complaint.

Fishing in a girl's hat was better than not fishing at all—but not much.

Fishing with Uncle Tot

☙

A huge hand shook my small shoulders. "Billy, get up," a deep voice said. "Let's go fishing." The hand and voice belonged to Colin Angus MacKay, my mother's brother, sarcastically nicknamed "Tot." I had been sleeping on the couch at my mother's family home, the same location at which I had experienced the humiliation of the girl's hat episode a year earlier. I was up quickly, got dressed, and without breakfast,

Fishing with My Uncles

followed Uncle Tot out the door, adrenaline surging through my five-year-old body.

In contrast to the weather of the year before, the early morning sun was bright behind us. Across the bay, the City of Duluth stretched along the steep hillside, roofs and multicolored sidings reflecting the sunlight. We walked into our long shadows down a short hillside to the edge of the water. It was late May, springtime in the North.

Tot's method of fishing was something I had never seen before or since. It takes a special environment to practice it, specifically a mix of water and railroad. The tracks had been built on a narrow causeway of gravel and cinders running parallel to the shore about a hundred feet out. The tracks thus enclosed a long narrow lagoon, connected under bridges at frequent intervals with the bay. Grass and small bushes grew from among the cinders and gravel between the wooden ties that supported the rails. Trains were apparently infrequent. When we reached the tracks, Tot quickly rigged up his tackle, which consisted of a 16-foot bamboo cane pole, about 20 feet of bait-casting line wrapped around the tip of the pole, a short wire leader, and finally the lure. This he pulled out of a small box in his pocket. It was a metal spoon, silver on one side and white with a red stripe on the other. A treble hook dangled menacingly from its tail end.

"What do we have for bait?" I asked.

"This is it," Tot said.

"But why do they bite on that thing? It doesn't look like a worm," I asked. The only bait I had ever used was earthworms.

"They think it's a minnow, I guess."

"Doesn't look like a minnow either," I said skeptically.

"They call it a Daredevil," he said.

With a graceless arc of the cane pole, he tossed the Daredevil into the water, and began walking slowly along the railroad tracks, holding the cane pole out over the lagoon. The Daredevil trailed about 15 to 20 feet behind the tip of the cane pole, a foot or two below the surface, flashing silver, red and white.

After walking for about five minutes, a fish hit the lure and Tot played it for about 30 seconds before he hauled up one of the biggest and certainly ugliest fish I had ever seen. It flopped and tossed itself violently between the rails, kicking up cinders and gravel in its effort to get back into the water, with the Daredevil rattling in its cheek. It seemed to me that that fish was at least three feet long, but I was small, and perhaps two-thirds that length may be more accurate. It was slender, green, and had oblong white spots along its body.

"What kind is it?" I asked Tot.

"That's a pike," Tot said, breathing more rapidly than he had been a few minutes before.

Fishing with My Uncles

It had a mouth full of sharply pointed teeth, such as I had never seen before, and although fish do not have very expressive faces, this one's expression could only be interpreted as mean. Tot killed the fish by bonking its head on the rail. Then he tied it on a stringer, tied the stringer to a shrub and placed the fish in the water to keep cool. We continued along the causeway for another half-hour. Tot caught no more fish that morning. We picked up the fish on our return trip.

I could hardly wait to get back to the house to show everyone that pike. Tot let me carry the trophy into the house. Everyone, now up, properly admired the fish. My mother fried it in butter, and we ate it for breakfast. That was my idea of a perfect morning. Tot had become my hero, much to my mother's dismay.

Despite the fact that I had held Tot in very high esteem, after catching that pike my mother never encouraged me to spend much time with him. My mother had become totally indoctrinated with the Protestant work ethic, and believed that one must earn what one gains through the sweat of one's brow, or at least through honest intellectual endeavor.

Tot had never subscribed to that idea. He happily sponged off the earnings of his father, and, whenever he could, his siblings. Tot had been in the military in World War I, and had received a minor non-combat wound. He was given a small pension to tide him through life.

After several years of scraping through, Tot discovered that his pension could be enhanced if he had a more permanent and visible injury, and so, my mother avows, he intentionally chopped off his little finger, claiming an accident. Thus his government pension went up, and he never had to work another day. He died sometime in the 1960s and was given a military burial. I believe my mother never shed a tear for him. But for me he remains a hero. That beautiful morning on St. Louis Bay with Uncle Tot left me with nothing but memories of what early mornings should be.

Catfish in the Bathtub
—Fishing with My Father

༗

My father's idea of idea of fishing differed greatly from that of his two brothers, Mutt and Loo, mainly in that he did not associate fishing with great physical exertion nor with getting lost, barking one's shins in streamside tangles, stumbling out of the woods long after dark, or coming home bleeding. He also looked different from Mutt and Loo, being taller, at five-foot-ten, by half-a-foot than they. His face was long and narrow, compared to his brothers' round faces, and his hair was straight rather than curly. One of his favorite quotes about Mutt and Loo's fishing behavior was from Bob Lyons, a musician, friend of the family and sometime fisherman: "I wouldn't fish with those guys if they fished off the harbor breakwater! They'd somehow get lost out there and not get home until the middle of the night."

But my father did fish, and before my brother was big enough to fish, he often took me with him. For three years in the late 1930s he taught instrumental music in Goldfield, a small farm town in north-central Iowa. One Saturday afternoon, while fishing by himself in the village park, he caught a huge catfish from

The Catfish in the Bathtub—Fishing with My Father

a deep hole in the Boone River. He carried it home across town with the fish flopping on a string. It became the talk of the town for a few days.

When he got home, the fish was still alive, as it was not a long walk across Goldfield, and catfish are not all that fussy about having to be underwater all the time. My mother felt sorry for the big fish, and so my dad put it into the bathtub, stopped the drain with a rubber plug on a chain, and poured in about 12 inches of water. The big fish swam about with the unflappable expression on its face that comes with being a catfish.

The question in my mind about how we were supposed to bathe was not addressed, nor was that of how long we expected to keep the fish alive. Although I had never tried taking a bath with a large catfish in the tub, given a preference, I thought I would rather bathe alone.

During the night, however, that problem was solved. The fish had entangled its tail in the chain and pulled the plug. We had not heard its struggles as we slept, and by morning it was dead. Even catfish cannot live six hours out of the water. It "committed suicide," my parents said.

"What does that mean?" I asked.

They told me, and to this day, when I hear of an account of a suicide, I think of that catfish.

We cooked and ate the fish for supper.

Fishing with My Uncles

It gets hot in Iowa in the summer. People there would say that on a hot summer night, if you listen carefully, you can hear the corn grow. Occasionally on a summer day, my father would take me fishing at Nelson's Pond, beside a gravel road somewhere near Goldfield. We would sit on the steep grassy bank in the shade of a clump of elm trees, and using worms for bait, throw out a couple of lines and usually catch a few bullheads.

Once, after feeling a bite, I jerked back, expecting to yank a bullhead up onto the bank. But instead something very, very powerful was on the other end of my line. My steel telescopic rod bent into a giant arc, and I started to slide down the bank. I tried to dig my heels into the grass, but I kept sliding toward the water as the huge fish thrashed and pulled. I could have let the fish have some line, but I knew nothing about "playing a fish," that is, keeping a taut line and gradually tiring the fish until it is exhausted and submits. I suppose I could have simply let go of my fishing rod, but I would rather get pulled into the water than let that big fish, or my rod, get away.

My father grabbed me around the waist. The fish kept pulling. I was getting stretched. My arms and shoulders started to hurt, but I was unwilling to let go of the rod.

Here I was, without realizing it, involved in the classic struggle that later in life I would read about in

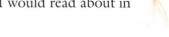

The Catfish in the Bathtub—Fishing with My Father

my American Literature classes: Man against beast. Melville's Captain Ahab and Moby Dick. Hemingway's Old Man and the Sea. Representing the human struggle against cosmic adversity, and – win or lose – somehow surviving the struggle and finding the meaning of life.

Apparently there is something heroic and symbolic in the story of a man on one end of the line and a great aquatic creature on the other. But in this case there was a small boy – me – in the middle. The thrashing of the great fish lasted only a few more moments before my line broke, and the beast disappeared into the murky depths of the pond, leaving bubbles and froth seething and popping on the surface. The rich and pungent smell of warm pond water remained. In a short while, the gray-green water became once again serene, and a cicada began to buzz in the elms.

"That was a big carp!" my father said, panting slightly. Both of our hearts were pounding, mine from the excitement of having a very large fish on my line, and his from nearly having to dive into the pond to save his son.

After moving to Marquette, Michigan, when I was six years old, my dad would now and then take me fishing at the harbor on Lake Superior. This was the town of his boyhood. It was his kind of fishing – less than half a mile from home, no branches to get

Fishing with My Uncles

your line tangled in, no biting insects, and you could cast your bait out and let the fish come to you. Some good-sized whitefish and trout could be caught off the breakwater or by the coal dock, where the water was deep. But a problem was that I could not swim. So we fished near the Cinder Pond, a small boat harbor where the water was only a few feet deep near shore.

In Iowa the ponds were small and shallow with murky water, and the land was flat or gently rolling. Now here we were on Lake Superior, virtually a freshwater ocean, so vast that you cannot see the Canadian shore, its water stretching to the northern horizon, crystal clear, cold, and its surface sparkling blue. Rocky wooded hills rose across the bay. In Iowa we always could catch enough bullheads for supper. Lake Superior was more beautiful, but less bountiful.

It was at the Cinder Pond that I believe my father developed a unique method of casting. He would bait the hook with a worm, sometimes with a silver spinner above the hook, and attach a couple of lead split-shot sinkers six to eight inches above the hook. Then he would lay the telescopic rod on the ground pointing directly away from the water. Taking about 20 to 25 feet of line off the reel, he would walk back and place the hook gently on the ground (which here happened to be mostly gravel, rock, and finely ground cinders from coal-burning vessels that once docked in

The Catfish in the Bathtub—Fishing with My Father

this location). He would then walk back to the rod at the water's edge, pick it up, and wing it sharply over his head toward the water, ducking slightly as the hook and sinker whistled past his ear. The terminal tackle would plop some distance out into the lake and quickly sink to the bottom. He preferred fishing on the bottom, rather than using a bobber. A bobber would drift in the wind or current and necessitate frequent reeling in and recasting – and casting in that style took some thought, time, effort and risk. A bobber also increased wind resistance in the cast, reducing its efficiency and increasing the chance that the hook would find the back of his neck.

Only now and then would we catch a fish, a pace much to my father's liking, as he did not think that fishing should keep one busy. We fished in the afternoon, occasionally catching a Menominee whitefish, a perch, a brook trout, a rainbow trout, or a four-inch long sculpin (which he called a dogfish). I do not remember bringing home more than one or two fish from the Cinder Pond, and none would be more than 10 inches long. But I remember my father, who tended to be a nervous and excitable person, being relaxed and content at those times, relieved to be back in his hometown in Michigan.

The summer before – 1938 – between Iowa school years, we had stayed for two months in a cozy gray canvas wall tent in a small clearing near the aban-

Fishing with My Uncles

doned town of Forestville, a few miles outside of Marquette. I was five years old, and my brother Dick was three or four months. My mother cooked our meals and sterilized Dick's diapers over a campfire. My father had a ten-foot wooden boat that he had built a few years before. He kept it tied up on the nearby reservoir, and he and I spent a lot of time fishing with worms for bluegills, perch and bass. It was not one of my mother's favorite summers. She seemed mostly to remember mosquitoes and the mice that had built a nest in our mattress.

Two years later we camped in the same tent for two months in a jack pine forest close to a Lake Superior beach, northwest of Marquette. One day my father took me in his rowboat along the shoreline to where we entered the swampy mouth of a stream. As we fished, I noticed a very large bird wading in the shallows. When we approached, it took wing, and as it flew over us I was awed by its size. Its wingspread seemed to be about ten feet, and it had a ferocious expression on its face. "That's a great blue heron," my father said. It was one of about a dozen birds that he knew the names of.

A few days later I had wandered alone down the beach. As I turned to head back toward our campsite, I saw, to my dismay, a great blue heron, probably the same one that my father and I had disturbed. It was flying only about 20 feet above the beach and direct-

The Catfish in the Bathtub—Fishing with My Father

ly toward me. Its beak looked long and sharp, and its yellow eyes were locked on me as it approached. I had forgotten to ask my father what great blue herons eat, and it occurred to me that they might eat small- to medium-sized children. I sank to my knees, then lay flat on the beach, barely daring to breathe or look up. I could hear the soft "whoosh, whoosh, whoosh" of its great wings, as my mouth went dry.

"Keep going, keep going," I pleaded silently and desperately to the bird. To my great relief the "whoosh, whoosh, whoosh" remained steady and then diminished as the monster bird passed overhead and beyond. I stayed perfectly still, except for peeking a little, until the bird went out of sight around a bend a mile or so down the beach.

That evening at supper around the campfire, I casually asked my dad, "Remember that bird we saw a couple of days ago? The great blue heron? What do they eat?"

"Oh, frogs and small fish, I guess. Why do you want to know?"

"Just wondering," I said, with some relief.

Fishing with My Uncles

Fishing with Uncle Lockie

I fished with Uncle Lockie only a few times. "Lockie" was Laughlin MacKay, my mother's older and respectable brother. He worked as an electric power plant operator in Superior, Wisconsin. He liked to catch big fish, such as bass and northern pike, out of lakes. Upon Lockie's invitation, in late July 1947, we packed up the family car, father, mother, brother and I, and we drove a couple of hundred miles to northwest Wisconsin, and moved into Lockie's cabin for a week with his wife, Stella, and his son, Lockie, Jr.

As we left Marquette in our black 1937 Ford, my father unwrapped a rum-soaked Crook cigar and lit it up. He smoked cigars only when we went on vacation. By the time the smoke from the cigar reached the back seat, he had already undergone his annual personality change — from a rather grumpy (but sometimes funny) conservative tightwad to a chuckling, joyful, flamboyant and generous philanthropist, feeling that "Now we are living! This is the life!" I've always associated the smell of cigar smoke with having a good time, although I never tried smoking a cigar myself.

When we crossed the Wisconsin border I men-

Fishing with Uncle Lockie

tioned that my bait-casting reel was not working very well. At the next town he stopped the car, we went into a sporting goods store, and I came out with a shiny new Bristol reel with level wind and quadrupling gears. If we hadn't been on vacation, it would have taken until my next birthday, nine months away, to get that reel.

As soon as we arrived at Lockie's cabin I ran down to the lake. I immediately went out on Lockie's dock, loaded my new reel onto my casting rod, and clipped a Hawaiian Wiggler onto my leader. A Hawaiian Wiggler was a popular lure at that time. It was about three inches long and featured a "grass skirt" made of multi-colored rubber strands, which some fish (that had never been to Hawaii) found irresistible. On the third cast with my new reel, I caught a 19-inch smallmouth bass, the largest one I've ever caught. "This is going to be great!" I thought, and it was.

My uncles MacKay (Tot and Lockie) were very large men, both well over 6 feet tall, and broad shouldered. When I first saw John Wayne in a movie, I thought this guy had been modeled after my uncle Lockie. Unlike my father's brothers, who liked to catch lots of small fish (brook trout) by wading in brush-covered streams, my mother's brothers liked to catch a few big fish from lakes. Lockie told us that a few weeks earlier he had caught a 16-pound northern pike.

Fishing with My Uncles

"What did you catch it on?" I asked.

"A perch," he replied.

During the week that followed, we fished, sometimes off the dock and sometimes from a boat. Lockie tried to teach Dick and me how to catch big pike. First you catch your bait, using a worm. Uncle Lockie took us out in his boat a short distance from his dock, where we caught and threw back several six- to eight-inch perch. (In Michigan we would usually keep eight-inch perch and eat them!)

Finally, Lockie hooked a good-sized perch. It was, in fact, a monster in our eyes, 12 inches, a beautiful fish. We hadn't caught perch any larger than that in our lives. Lockie then hooked the perch through the back with a giant hook, attached a plastic bobber about the size of a pint milk bottle about five feet above the hook, and cast it out about 15 yards from the boat. The bobber and perch sort of spiraled out and landed with two big splashes. Lockie settled down to watch the bobber and wait for a pike to take his perch.

The bobber frequently went underwater for a period of up to a minute as that perch was strong enough to go nearly anywhere he pleased as long as he did not have to pull the anchored boat we were in. Meanwhile, Dick, Lockie, Jr., and I were catching small perch and bluegills.

After watching Uncle Lockie's bait for a half-hour

or so, I asked, "How do you know if you get a bite?"

"The bobber goes under for a little while, then comes up and stops. That means that the pike is adjusting the perch in its mouth to swallow it. When the bobber moves steadily away, the pike has probably taken the perch well into his mouth, and if you jerk on the line with your rod, you will probably hook the pike."

This time, however, no monster pike took his perch. But Uncle Lockie seemed quite content to watch the movements of a 12-inch perch towing his bobber about, and to see his son and nephews catch a few small perch, while awaiting the attack of the Wisconsin version of Moby Dick.

By the end of the week in Wisconsin, Lockie had not caught a monster pike on his 12-inch perch. That perch eventually got tired so we ate it. Dick and I had caught several perch and a few small bass.

The fishing highlight of the trip for me, however, was an evening trip to a small nearby body of water called Web Lake. There were patches of lily pads on the lake, and the hills around the lake were covered with fruiting blueberry bushes and some scattered oaks. My mother, Uncle Lockie, Dick and I enjoyed a lingering summer sunset.

Lockie rowed his boat, and I cast a popper with my fly rod. The bass loved it, and so did I. They would hit the popper and, as largemouth bass do,

Fishing with My Uncles

jump out of the water shaking their heads trying to free the hook. We caught eight or ten one evening and released all of them.

My father fished only seldom during that week in Wisconsin. The previous owners of the cabin had left several items of furniture and, to my father's delight, a musical instrument called an Autoharp. My father had a Bachelor's Degree in music, and although he no longer taught it for a living, he continued to play music as an avocation. At the end of the week my father had learned to play a few tunes on the Autoharp. This was the beginning of a five-year fascination with zithers and Autoharps, on which he learned to play numerous pieces, bringing musician friends and relatives to our house to produce pleasant music and good friendships.

A few years after our fishing visit to Wisconsin, Lockie, young Lockie and Stella came to visit us in Marquette for two days. On the second day Lockie bought a Michigan fishing license, and most of the family went fishing at Caribou Lake, about 30 miles east of town. For some reason, I decided to stay at home. Late in the afternoon I rode my bike out to the Sleeping River, about two miles from our house. I fished for about a half-hour and caught what for me was a good bass — a 17-inch smallmouth. I took the bass home to eat it, and the rest of the folks showed up in the early evening. They had not caught a fish large enough to bother to keep.

Uncle Lockie was actually jealous, and he immediately wanted to go to where I had caught the bass. Within minutes we were in his car, headed for the Sleeping. We spent the remaining hour of daylight casting lures in an effort to entice another decent smallmouth. No luck. In a way, I felt guilty that Lockie did not catch a decent fish in Michigan, but I also felt just a bit smug that I was able to catch a very respectable fish, within bicycling range of home, when the rest of the folks had traveled about 60 miles and brought home none.

Fishing with My Uncles

Just Loo and I

🦆

Gardner's Creek is only a few miles from town. In its lower reaches, kids fishing have worn paths along its banks. But a few miles farther up, beyond the impenetrable cedar swamp and the dense alder thickets, it tumbles down from the granite hills, water the color of light sherry wine; and there are no footprints or paths along its bank. It is only three to five feet wide. This is the kind of place my uncles would frequent from June through August. There were not many fish and they were not big, but they were wild and it took skill and tolerance of insects and barked shins to catch them.

One day, in late June, my uncle Loo and I had slogged through the swamps and tall grass, and then gone farther, fishing as we went against the current. At one spot the stream ran swift and shimmering through a patch of sunshine across a short stretch of multi-colored gravel, and then dove beneath the roots of a cedar, deepening and slowing. Dead branches of fallen alder swept by the current all but blocked the hole among the cedar roots — a perfect spot for a trout to hide. I lowered my worm-baited hook into the stream above the alder twigs and let the stream carry it into the darkness of shadows and roots.

If a brook trout is going to bite, it usually does so right away. One did. Tug, tug, tug! I yanked back, and felt the trout, strong, surging against the rod and line, but it had already entangled itself among the submerged alder twigs.

I could see it struggling and twisting, his orange belly, red-sides and speckled back flashing in and out of the sunshine. He was big, at least for me — probably eight or nine inches long. I wanted that fish. I wanted to show it to my mother when I got home and to have her fry it for me for supper. All I had to do was get that fish out of there. So I pulled extra hard. My steel telescopic rod bent, then sprang back-

Fishing with My Uncles

wards, sending my hook and sinker high above my head. The sinker spun several times around an alder branch and the hook clasped the line. I had had one quick glimpse of the trout before it had found sudden freedom and quickly disappeared into the shadows of the stream. A cloud of silty dust drifted down in the current and settled to the bottom.

I would not see that fish again, and of course I would not eat it. And now my hook and line were high in a tree. I pulled and yanked, but the hook would not come loose. Mosquitoes that I hadn't noticed before were biting my ears, neck and legs through my pants. There was mud in my shoes. I started to cry.

Loo heard me and came down. He was a small man with dark curly hair. He laughed a bit when he saw me. I wasn't offended. It was a gentle laugh and it reassured me that the situation wasn't all that grave. He took my rod, broke off the line and showed me how to tie a new hook on and how to bite the sinker to clinch it on the line.

"There'll be more fish upstream," he said. "There's a lot of 'em in here."

We moved on upstream, sneaking and plunking our worms beneath logs. Loo caught three "keeper" trout (longer than seven inches) and put them in his canvas shoulder bag with some ferns that he had moistened in the stream to keep the trout cool.

Just Loo and I

Near its headwaters, Gardner's Creek flows through a sphagnum bog. A bog is formed by vegetation. Spongy sphagnum moss and several woody shrubs combine to make a floating mat. As we reached the bog we became aware that the sun was no longer shining and it was getting dark. Huge thunder clouds swirled and climbed into the sky, and others swept low over the trees. Loo said that sometimes the fish really bite when it rains, and he started to make his way out across the bog toward the open water of the slowly flowing stream. The bog was quaking with our weight, sending slow-moving ripples outward, causing the shrubs 15 feet away from us to quiver. One might imagine walking on a giant water bed covered lushly with mosses, pitcher plants and shrubs called leatherleaf and sweet gale. But, unlike a water bed, the covering of a bog varies in thickness, and the water beneath it also varies in depth.

Suddenly the dark sky opened up. Great fat drops of cold rain pelted us as we felt our way over the spongy bog. Loo found a thin spot and learned that the water in a bog indeed can be over a short man's head. I was scared as I watched him sink and then start paddling and struggling to pull himself back up on the bog mat. But he laughed as he emerged with some unidentified small aquatic plant hanging from his right ear and was chuckling as he rolled himself over among the sphagnum and sweetgale, so I wasn't

Fishing with My Uncles

afraid.

Despite the fun that Loo was having, he decided that we should probably hike back to the car and call it a day. "Maybe some other day," Loo said.

I remember crying three times that day, twice when my line got tangled, and once when I lost the trout. I almost cried when I slipped and fell over a log and landed on my hand and my face got scratched, but I didn't.

When he dropped me off at home my mother asked him, "Well, how was Billy?"

"Good," Loo said. "He only bawled once, when he got his line tangled."

We would get other chances to test his theory that fish really bite in the rain. And we did, many times.

You Ain't No Six-Foot-One

❦

This story was told to me by my uncle Loo. Sometime in the late 1920s, a guest staying at my grandparents' house on Pine Street in Marquette asked Mutt if he would take him fishing. Mutt was eager to oblige, but it was early in the summer, it was Sunday, and he had not yet purchased a fishing license. Another guest at the house, a tall man named Moxy Bielingberg, said he had a Michigan fishing license and that he was not planning to fish that afternoon, so Mutt could borrow his. Mutt divested himself of all other identification, and he and the house guest headed northward for an afternoon of brook trout fishing.

They fished a few hours and did well. In late afternoon as they approached their car, baskets loaded with trout for supper, they found a man waiting for them. He asked about the fishing, and Mutt and his companion showed him a dozen legal-sized brook trout, well within the limit of 15 each. The man then showed Mutt and his friend his Game Warden badge, and asked to see their fishing licenses. To himself Mutt thought, "Boy, I'm glad I thought to borrow Moxy's license."

The warden routinely checked Mutt's compan-

Fishing with My Uncles

ion's license, approved it, then checked Mutt's. He scanned the license—weight, age, height, residence, etc. and was about ready to approve and hand it back to Mutt. Then suddenly the warden looked at the license once again and at Mutt's five-foot-two-inch stature and said, "You ain't no six-foot-one. You're gonna have to pay the fine now, or we're goin' to jail."

Mutt had no money, and his companion said he didn't either.

About a half-hour later, the phone rang at the Pine Street house in Marquette. My father answered, and started to chuckle. It was Mutt in jail in Ishpeming, still with the warden. "Can you bring twenty-five bucks up so I can go home?" Mutt pleaded. Everyone in the house got a laugh. My father drove up to Ishpeming, and 45 minutes later, Mutt was free.

The adventure was almost worth the 25-dollar fine, but there must be some lesson about borrowing a fishing license from someone who is nearly a foot taller than you.

I do not know what happened to the trout.

The Knot

❦

It was summer and Sunday and I was 10 years old. I sat on the grass impatiently amusing myself by practicing the most difficult maneuver in the ritualistic game of jack-knife. The shadow of the small oak tree that my father and I had planted a few years before fluttered on our front lawn. I stuck the knife into the grass at an angle, laid my leg out in front of the knife, put my first two fingers under the handle, and gave it a good flip. It traveled in an end-over-end arc with its shiny blade flashing above my leg, hit the ground and skidded on its back a few feet. If it goes right it sticks in. I reached over, picked up the knife and tried it again. I wished my father would get out of bed so we could go fishing.

Fishing with My Uncles

Through the screen door I could hear my mother rattling breakfast pans, turning water on and off, and once in a while yelling, "Thomas! Come on. Get up. It's too nice a day to spend in bed." My mother liked fishing too. But this never worked. My father would just mumble and roll over. He got up only when he felt like it, and on Sundays in summer he never felt like it until noon.

My brother Dick, who was only five years old, was lying on the living room floor looking at the Sunday funny papers. I could hear him kicking his toes on the floor now and then. A car rattled slowly by on the gravel street beside our house. A few houses up the block I saw the Goldsworthys coming home from Mass, four girls in frilly dresses. It seemed that in the summertime the only ones who went to church were Catholics and women who sang in the Protestant choirs. Between the Fourth of July and Labor Day, the Protestant churches had few faithful parishioners. Apparently their kindly God would look the other way, not noticing the empty pews, for summer in Northern Michigan did not last long, and one of His fine Sunday mornings was not to be spent indoors.

But my father was not a churchgoer, and he did not consider a Sunday morning indoors wasted, especially if it was wasted in bed.

I had gotten everything ready. On Saturday I had dug a can full of worms. I had counted each one as I

The Knot

plucked its slippery, wriggling form from the shovels full of black soil among the alders, and now they lay calmly bunched beneath the dirt in the bottom of the silvery can on the floor of our black 1937 humpbacked Ford. Four telescopic fishing rods with reels and lines and dried up worms on the hooks were already in the car on the shelf by the rear window, and a canvas shoulder bag containing extra hooks, sinkers, spinners and a trolling spoon lay on the back seat. Two oars, which did not fit in the trunk, sprawled diagonally from the corner of the back floor to the brown upholstered ceiling. I had even gotten my brother's old crib mattress out of the back shed and had managed to slide it onto the top of the car. The mattress served as a pad on which the boat would rest. I knew the routine well, because we went fishing nearly every Sunday.

    It seemed to me that it was at least four in the afternoon when my father finally got up, but it was close to noon. He came to the kitchen in his underwear, as he always did, sat at his place, and peered out the window above the kitchen table allowing the full realization of his arousal to steep into his consciousness. As my mother poured his coffee I heard him say, "Well, what do you people have planned for today?" He delivered this question, which he asked every Sunday, in such a manner as to make my mother feel that he was being bullied by his family on his own holiday.

Fishing with My Uncles

His behavior was probably influenced by several family comic strips, in which the father was subordinate to all of the other family members. My father knew that today was Sunday and that meant going fishing; and he knew that he liked fishing as well as the rest of us, but he had to pretend he did not. Otherwise he would be allowed no privacy on Sunday mornings, and it was no pretense that he liked sleeping better than did his wife and two kids.

When my father had finished his breakfast, a cigarette, going to the toilet, another cup of coffee, getting dressed, and every other stall he could think of, he faced the outside world of sunshine and shadows and an impatient 10-year-old son buoyed by the tangible evidence of his father upright and moving, greeting him at the side door as he came out.

He was wearing what he always wore for fishing: a dark blue work shirt, loosely fitting bib overalls, high-cut black work shoes with hooks instead of holes for the laces near the top, and a blue-and-white-striped denim railroad cap. He appeared tall for he was thin, and his long face was accented by a central point of straying dark hair left stranded by an otherwise receding hairline, now hidden beneath his cap. Deep wrinkles radiated from the outer corners of his eyes. These had evolved, I imagined, from squinting ahead through flying cinders down the rails and back past the long strings of boxcars to catch the signals of

The Knot

brakemen as he leaned out the window of the cab of his engine.

I followed him around to the back of the house where the boat lay on two planks in the shade. It was partly filled with water to keep the boards from drying and shrinking. It was a dark green boat, only ten feet long with a flat bottom. My father had built the boat himself before I was born. He had hewn the stem with a butcher knife from the kitchen drawer. The thin, almost delicate cedar planking had been fastened to the ribs with neatly counter-sunk brass screws, puttied and smoothly painted over leaving only the faintest round impressions to honor the presence of his craftsmanship. It was a boat made to be propelled by rowing, and the brass sockets for the oarlocks were smooth and shiny inside from the friction of the turning oarlocks. My father took pride in the fact that no sputtering outboard engine had ever pushed it around a lake. The paint of the stern was unmarred by bare little circles that would have been made by the harsh clamps of a motor. The boat was a part of our family.

We tilted it up on one side, my father near the stern and I near the bow. The week-old brownish water spilled out with a rush, and I stood on my toes as the puddle surrounded my sneakers. But already the water was seeping into the dry sandy soil, and my father said, "All right, let it down again."

Next my father went around the boat and took a

grip on the rail. I did likewise on my side. We lifted it a foot or so off the ground and carried it to the car on the street. We readjusted our grips and lifted the boat upside down onto the mattress. The perspiration of exertion and of a summer's day moistened my father's face.

Dick came out of the house and got into the car to sit in the heat and pretend he was driving while he waited for the end of the seemingly endless and unnecessary chores that big people attended to. I got into the car with Dick to fool around while we were waiting. My mother stayed inside the house to finish cleaning up or whatever she did, and my father went to get the two ropes from the basement.

He returned shortly, the spiraled coils of brown rope dangling from his hands. He had always tied the ropes himself, for the boat had to be fastened securely to the car. There was no room for error. A carelessly loose rope and a bad bump in the rough road to the lake could toss the boat to sudden splintered destruction, and the afternoon, and the summer, would be spoiled. Often I had watched my father tie the ropes, noting the careful skill with which he united boat and car.

As he neared the car he said, "Billy, come out here. I'll show you how to tie down the boat." I stepped down out of the car trying to show only small interest. New responsibility must be accepted with

The Knot

dignity. As I turned to close the car door, the thought came upon me that I was being entrusted with a portion of the family happiness. I was old enough now. I was 10. I had to learn this, and I had to learn it well. "Watch how I put the rope on," he said, but I need not have watched this first part because I had seen him do it many times, and I knew how to do it. Reaching up and under the boat he threaded the rope between the rail and the gunwale just behind the second rib, first on one side then the other. Next he walked out in front to pull the two ends of the rope even. He promptly returned to the side, passing the rope again between the rail and gunwale so it made a loop around the rail, and then he did the same thing on the other side. The procedure was repeated with the second rope in the back, and the ropes were ready to be crossed over and tied to the sturdy black braces that held the shiny bumper a safe six inches away from the fenders and grille. I knew how to do that much. It was the knot that I did not know. My father's sure fingers had always wound the rope into the knot so quickly that I could not follow his movements. Sometimes after we had arrived at the lake and as I had untied the knot I had tried to follow its course backward so that I might reconstruct it by putting my mind into reverse. But it was like trying to learn to knit by unraveling a sweater, and I had become discouraged.

Fishing with My Uncles

I stood close to my father to watch, hoping he would not see my admiring grin as he pulled the right rope snug against the left bumper brace.

"Twice around," he told me. "The second loop overlaps the first so it binds it in place."

Now it was time to tie the knot. About a foot above the bumper he crossed the end over the tight descending line and passed it down through the oblong loop. He pulled this part tight. Then he passed the rope directly over the junction that had just been formed and through the loop again. "Now pull this up tight until you feel it snap into place," he said, handing me the rope. I pulled hard on the taut end and felt a sudden inch of slack, and then firmness as the two overlapping rings of rope locked themselves tightly into place. My father then took back the rope and secured the loose end over the locked coils with a half bow like the one I tied on my shoe when one end of the lace was too short. And the knot was tied. It was not difficult, I thought, quickly reviewing the steps in my mind.

Then we moved over to the right bumper brace. I hoped that I would be asked to tie this one because I wanted to show my father how fast I had learned the knot. My father handed me the rope. "Here," he said, "You do this one." I took the rope and pulled downward until it was straight and tight. I began to pass it over the bumper brace when my father stopped me.

The Knot

"Wait a minute. Always put it around left to right."

I considered his suggestion for a moment. If I was making a circle around the bumper brace, no matter which way I passed the rope it was going from left to right. It depended on whether the point of reference was the top or the bottom of the brace. I proceeded on a trial-and-error basis and my next trial must have been left to right because I was allowed to continue.

After wrapping it twice around the bumper brace I started the knot. I crossed the end over the descending line about a foot above the brace and passed it through the loop when my father said, "No, no. Take it back. Always start out going from left to right and cross the rope over away from you."

"Why?" I asked, but this was not the right question because I still did not understand the left to right business and now I had the further complicating factor of "away from you." In tying a knot, I thought, what goes away from you must also come toward you or else you cannot make it tie. I desperately hoped for some clarification in my father's answer.

"So it comes out that the knot is easier to tie for a right-handed person," he replied. No help there. It had all seemed so easy when he had shown me how. I was enraged at myself for having ignored these important details in the lesson. I thought that my father must have been thinking, "Ten years old and not capable of learning to tie a simple knot." Tears of

Fishing with My Uncles

anger and frustration welled into my eyes and I had to struggle to keep them from spilling over. My father, with patient instructions guided my blurred hands through the motions of tying the knot on the remaining ropes, but I could not learn it now. The pebbles in the gravel of the street swam dizzily before my eyes, and the smells of hot pine needles, roast beef and my father's clean overalls probed incoherently at my consciousness.

I tried to concentrate silently on holding back the tears, a battle that I had fought with myself many times before. A blink at the wrong moment or even a word spoken could start the tears on their shiny salty path down my cheeks and thereby record a double failure for the day. Tears of 10-year-olds must be dammed as urgently as those of adults, but 10-year-olds have not had as much practice, and success comes less often. But the day was warm, and when my father went back to the house I stood there by the car, and the tears evaporated from my eyes before spilling over. Only a smarting sensation remained, and I blinked it away. But the sun could not evaporate my self-disgust, nor could I blink away my failure to learn the knot. Much as I had tried to hide them, my tears must have been noticed by my father, and the thought of this was piled heavily upon my other failure.

In the days that followed, while my father was at work, I spent determined hours in our back yard. My

The Knot

mother's clothesline had a long loose end. I sat in a canvas lawn chair near the clothes post wrapping the rope around the wooden arm of the chair pretending it was the bumper brace, trying all possible combinations of twists and turns and loops that can be done with a rope. Finally on Wednesday, just before noon, I tied the knot. And I began to tie and untie and retie the rope as fast as I could, until I was late for lunch, and the patience of my mother had neared the spanking threshold. As I practiced the knot later I figured out that "left to right" referred to the top of the circle and that "away from you" means away from you first and then toward you. After a few days I could tie the knot every way possible, left or right-handed, starting out right to left or left to right, or by bringing the end toward me first or away from me. I could tie it with rope, string, and even my shoelace. I had, in every sense of the word, mastered the knot.

But in all the rest of that summer's Sunday afternoons my father never again asked me to tie the ropes. I knew, however, that my chance would eventually come, and with a patience that I found surprising in myself, I waited through the whole winter.

Early the next summer my father showed the knot to me only once, and of course on my first try I quickly duplicated his demonstration. He did not say anything, but I knew he must have been thinking, "Boy, he really learns fast for an eleven-year-old," and I felt sneakily proud of it.

After that he would tie the front ropes, and I tied the back ones all by myself. By August he had even stopped coming around to the back to pull on the ropes to test their tightness and examine the knots. I could do the job, and he knew it.

Then the summers went by, each one a little faster than the last. On Sunday mornings my father would sleep, Dick and I would put the boat on the car, and I would tie the ropes. As we would drive to Carver Lake the crossed ropes would vibrate tightly, and the prow of the boat upside down on top would shade the windshield from the occasional flashes of sunlight that found their way to the road through the birches and pines.

Once while fishing, my mother hooked a big pike that flopped on the floor of the boat while my father tried to club it with an oar, which he did eventually after several swats. When we looked up after the confusion, we saw a black bear philosophically watching us from the shore. These were happy times.

Then I went away, to college and summer jobs far from home, two years in the U.S. Army, and after that, graduate school in Maine. But never did I feel that I had moved away from Michigan permanently. And the knot stayed with me, too.

I often used an Old Town canoe to study waterfowl, and the ropes which held the canoe to the car

The Knot

were tied always with the same knot. The knot's utility seemed to justify the memories, which so often entwined themselves among its loops. I always insisted on tying the ropes myself, lest someone in careless ignorance throw a pair of hurried half hitches or a granny knot. One time a friend apologized to me for not tying the canoe down, "I would have tied it," he said. "But I suppose you know your own hitch and like it best." I proudly accepted his respect.

Letters from home told me that my father had given the boat to a friend who had to tear out the bottom planking as the cedar had finally rotted. He had replaced it with a single sheet of plywood. The boat just wasn't the same.

Then one summer I came home. I was 27 years old and Dick was 22. Once again, on Sunday morning I could feel the impatient anticipation of a family-fishing trip to Carver Lake. My father, now riding a crest of post-war prosperity for railroad workers, had bought, not built, a new boat for the Sunday fishing trips. The new boat was the same length as the old one, but it was made of fiberglass, its color was red and white and it was very wide, very deep and somehow heavier than the old boat. Dick's old crib mattress had been replaced atop the car by metal racks that were barely wide enough to hold the new boat. And of course the car was new, too, a dark blue Plymouth with not a bumper brace to be found.

Fishing with My Uncles

When the red and white boat had been loaded on the car with more struggles than I could ever recall with the old boat, my father produced from the basement, to my dismay, a five-horsepower outboard engine. He put the oily motor into the trunk along with a smelly red can of gasoline and a tin of worms purchased from a local bait dealer.

He and I passed the ropes over the boat, and I began to tie my end to the metal rack. My father left his end loose and came around the car. He stood beside me for a moment watching, then asked, "Didn't we used to tie a certain knot here? I don't remember it. How did that thing go again?"

I had learned that the name of the knot was the taut-line knot, and I showed him how I tied it.

Mutt's Fly Rod

✍

When Mutt went off to war in 1941, he received a gift of a brand new split bamboo fly rod from Local 218, American Federation of Musicians. He had served as president of the Local for several years. I had not realized that there was a perfectly good fly rod, stored at my grandparents' house on Pine Street, and I believe it had never been used. Such an item was not available for sale anywhere during the war.

My friend Jack Parent and I had become interested in fly-fishing. We were tying our own flies, under the tutelage of Don MacPherson, a middle-aged man and skilled fly-fisherman whom Jack had befriended. We found out that it is possible to cast a fly with a steel telescopic rod, but not very well. The telescopic rods had only three or four guides on them, and sometimes one of the sections would twirl around, causing the line to twist around the rod, making it difficult to play the line out while casting.

My grandfather, learning that I wanted to take up fly-fishing, decided that Mutt would not mind if I borrowed his fly rod. I couldn't wait to try it. I stepped out the side door and put the rod together. I was going to practice casting in the yard with a genuine fly rod. The metal ferrules fit together perfectly

Fishing with My Uncles

and the rod felt very light. Excitedly, I attached a reel with line (not a real fly fishing line, just a standard bait-casting line) with leader on it and strung line and leader through the guides. I had tied a barrel knot to connect line and leader. The knot got caught in one of the guides. I gave a little tug to free the knot, but the line did not slide through. So I gave it a somewhat heavier tug, bending the rod. Suddenly I heard a sharp snap, and felt the rod break in two at one of the ferrules.

I had broken Mutt's beautiful brand new fly rod before he had ever had a chance to use it. And there he was out there in the Pacific, fighting the Japanese, and here I was, 11 years old at home breaking his brand new fly rod. No one had the heart to write to Mutt and tell him that his nephew had broken his one and only fly rod.

Mutt did not come directly home after the war had ended in 1945, which was okay with me. He spent about a year in Wyoming, doing road construction work. But in the summer of 1946, he returned to Marquette, and I had to face him.

After he had recounted his adventures over the past few years, I had to tell him, "Mutt," I said, "You're not going to like this, but do you remember the fly rod that you got from the Musicians' Union?"

"Yeah," he said. "What about it?"

"Well, I sort of borrowed it, and thought you

wouldn't mind, but it broke the first time I strung it up."

Mutt broke out in a grin, chuckled and said, "I never liked that thing, anyhow. You can have it." But I already knew the rod couldn't be fixed. It never saw a lake or a stream.

Split bamboo rods became available in 1946. One early summer day my grandfather showed up with a long, slender package and handed it to me, saying, "Here's something for you." It was a brand new split bamboo fly rod, a Montague Flash. I got my reel, threaded the line carefully through the guides, and made a few casts in the front yard. That rod lasted me about six years. Mutt's easy forgiveness stayed with me longer.

Fishing with My Uncles

Embryology of a Fly Fisherman

🖎

My world of fishing was not solely influenced by my family. At age 11, I discovered sportsmen's magazines. Before I was old enough to join the Boy Scouts, I was allowed to attend the Monday night meetings with my older friends.

One Monday evening in January, a man named Perry Hatch came to our scout meeting and gave a demonstration of fly casting. We met in what was called the "Little Gym" at the college. Mr. Hatch was using a split bamboo fly rod. (I believe that all fly rods at the time were made of Tonkin cane, from the Orient, carefully split and glued into a hexagonal cross section, gracefully tapering from the cork handle grip to the tip top.) He said he was using his old fly line because there would be some sand from our shoes on the gym floor, and he did not want to damage a good line. As he cast, I admired the graceful arc that the line made in the air, and Mr. Hatch's ability to put the fly into a small circle 25 to 30 feet away on the floor. Jack Parent and I seemed to be the only ones awed by the demonstration. We wanted to do that—not on the gymnasium floor, but in a real stream.

After the scout meetings my friends and I would stop at Bittner's Store and buy Twinkies, Pepsi Cola

Embryology of a Fly Fisherman

and an outdoor magazine. The store handled only four of the six or seven of those published in 1944-47. When there were five Mondays in a month, I suffered what might be called mild magazine withdrawal symptoms from having to go for a whole week without reading about how Joe caught five 16-pound Atlantic salmon in New Brunswick, 800 miles to the east, or how good the fishing was in the Yellowstone River, 800 miles to the west.

It never occurred to us that the authors of these fine magazine articles might embellish the truth a bit for dramatic effect. It seemed that there was a pattern, in which things would not go well for a while, but nearly invariably they would end up catching a 20-pound muskellunge, getting a limit of large bluegills, or when hunting, shooting a 10-point buck on the last day of the season.

But there were some good writers. Ed Zern was my idol. He wrote funny fishing books, and was employed by Nash automobiles to write good and amusing advertisements for them. In 1946, just after World War II, Nash had come out with a model in which the seats folded down into a bed. I was 13 years old then, and I could hardly wait until I would be old enough and have money enough to buy one of those. I would picture myself packing the car with groceries, and a blanket or two, fishing a different stream each day, and curling up every night in my Nash for a week

Fishing with My Uncles

or two at a time.

Unfortunately, by the time I could afford a car, most of those Nash dream cars were no longer running. My grandmother, who also lived in Marquette, owned one of those. She was the typical little old lady who used her Nash only to go to church and the grocery store. She sold the car when I was living in Canada. After 15 years, I missed my chance at my dream car. But I did get to meet Ed Zern.

When I was in my late 40s, I attended a Wildlife Conference in Portland, Oregon. One of the speakers was Zern. After his speech I sought him out, and we chatted. We discussed an article he had written, critical of modern gadgets, and the emphasis on catching large fish. He confessed that if he were to write the article again, he would modify it.

"Why?" I asked.

"Well," he said, "Maybe a little less chip on the shoulder."

I was awed, just as I was when I was 13. Just to talk with him was an experience of a lifetime. He was a bright and serious man, with true concerns about the future of fishing and hunting and the fate of the environment upon which the future of this planet depends.

The Quarry Pond

❦

Every fisherman associates intimately with water and is therefore aware of the possibility of drowning. Even those who fish in shallow but swift streams know of the chance of slipping on a smooth, wet rock and tumbling out of control in a rapids. The tops of boots or waders can catch in the current and drag you along. Each year, we read of fishermen who drown, and sometimes a drowning hits close to home.

Sonny Babich had been a quiet boy. He lived on East Park Street, two blocks from my home and near where most of my friends lived. His parents, Slavic immigrants, kept to themselves. When he was four or five years old, Sonny, whose real name was Edward, had been burned. His neck, chest and arms were badly scarred, with yellowish wrinkled skin. The story of his burns was that he and another boy or two had been playing with matches, and somehow Sonny's shirt had caught fire. That was all we knew. Nobody, not even the adults who may have known how it had happened, would talk about it. And Sonny was deeply embarrassed.

Sonny went to school, but he did not make friends. As several of us who were all about Sonny's age would play softball on Park Street, he would often

Fishing with My Uncles

watch from his yard. We would invite him to play, but he would not accept, sometimes staying in his yard playing with his two older sisters, Carol ("Canny") and Lorraine. Sometimes he would just shake his head and go quietly into his house.

His father seemed bitter toward all other boys, and by all indications, hated all of us—Jack, Rich, George, Bob, Ron, Jim, Charlie, Paul and me. He was a machine operator at a local factory. In late afternoons, after work, he would sometimes tend a few flowers inside the picket fence which enclosed the small front yard around his small white house. His wife was seldom seen. Occasionally the ball we were playing with would go foul or be thrown errantly into his yard. Usually it would stay there until after dark, when one of us would get up the courage to sneak through the gate to retrieve it. We feared that Mr. Babich would catch us and whip us. It seemed that he blamed all of us for Sonny's burns.

But in the summer of 1944, when I was 11, Sonny began to overcome his shyness. He would join us in our ball games on the street, and we began to call him Eddie. Of course he was not a good ball player—he had never done it before—but we tried to help him, and once in a while he would reach first base or catch a fly ball. A couple of times that summer he even walked to the beach with us, where we would swim in the cold Lake Superior water and lie in the sand, as

The Quarry Pond

beach-goers do the world around. Eddie did not learn to swim. He mostly stayed on the beach, keeping his shirt on.

Sonny's father began to loosen. Once, when he was weeding his peonies beside the porch, the ball went into his yard. We got up our courage, and I think Ron asked, "Mr. Babich, could we come and get our ball?"

"Humph," he snorted. "No. You keep tat ball outa my yard," he grouched.

I think we said something like, "Please?"

Mr. Babich walked purposefully a few steps over to the softball, picked it up, and awkwardly flung it towards us scowling, "Here's da got-tammed ball." It sailed way over our heads and into the yard across the street. "Whoops," he said, and returned to his weeding.

That "whoops" was the kindest thing we had ever heard him say.

By August, Eddie had been allowed to go fishing with us a couple of times, and he enjoyed it. One afternoon Eddie, Jack and Rich rode their bikes to the Quarry Pond at the south edge of town to fish for perch and bluegills. For some reason, Ron, Charlie and I had decided that day to fish in Three Lakes north of town. The Quarry Pond occupied an abandoned rock quarry from which, decades ago, large blocks of sandstone had been chiseled to become the walls of hotels, churches and office buildings of the city. Upon abandonment, the pit had filled with water. In some places the shore sloped gently, but in others, the banks were nearly vertical, disappearing into the water, which was known to be deep. A few small ledges, supporting scattered saplings of white birch and pin cherries, broke the steepness of the banks.

Standing on one of those ledges, Rich began to catch a few bluegills, some of them eight to nine inches long, which is large for bluegills. Jack and Eddie came along the shore to join him. As they attempted to scramble toward the water, Eddie lost his footing, and went skidding down the bank, grabbing at the small trees, but nothing held him back. As he slid he had rolled and his fishing line had wrapped around his legs and ankles. Soon he was in the water, arms flailing, panic in his eyes.

Jack dove in to help. He caught Eddie, but Eddie grabbed desperately at Jack, clutching at whatever he could—clothing, arms, and hands. But Eddie's head kept going under water. He came up coughing a couple of times, arms flailing and grasping. Once he pulled the collar off Jack's shirt.

"Don't pull me down, Eddie!" Jack shouted. "I'll get you out." Then Eddie disappeared. Jack dove and found Eddie once and then once more, but now Eddie was getting heavy and Jack was getting tired.

The Quarry Pond

He, too, had taken some water into his lungs. He could no longer hang on to Eddie without both of them drowning. Jack crawled out onto the bank.

He caught his breath then tried diving where Eddie had disappeared. Three times he tried, but could find no sign of his young friend. Rich, who was not a good swimmer, could do nothing but keep himself from falling in. He could only encourage Jack.

Jack, panting, finally asked Rich, "What are we going to do?"

What do you do when you are 13 years old and your friend has just disappeared under water? They got on their bikes and headed home as fast as they could go. Passing through downtown they told a policeman, who did not understand them, and they sped on the last six blocks home. Jack's father called the police.

An hour and a half later a Coast Guard Rescue Squad pulled Eddie's body from the Quarry Pond. They worked at artificial respiration for over an hour. At 8 p.m. the County Coroner arrived, and pronounced Eddie Babich dead.

I learned about it an hour later when I went to visit the Wilsons. Bob's mother told me that Eddie had drowned. I had never known anyone so well or so young who had died. I did not cry right away, but I had trouble talking, and I wanted to cry. It was hard to accept that death was forever, and that it could

Fishing with My Uncles

happen to someone so quickly and so young. When I went home and told my parents, I broke down sobbing. My mother hugged me.

The headline on page two of the local daily paper, *The Mining Journal*, August 26, 1944, read impersonally, "Youth Drowns in Quarry Pool." Eddie, it said, was 13 years old, two years older than I. I had thought that he was younger.

All of us, the street softball players, were named as pall bearers. The sharing of grief had apparently brought forgiveness. Before the funeral we were invited into the Babich's kitchen for cookies. Eddie's mother and sisters talked with us, and his father quietly seemed to approve of us being there nervously chatting. They all knew how hard Jack had tried to save their son and brother.

We carried the casket from the funeral parlor to the hearse, and again from the hearse to the grave, choking back our tears. The hearse driver asked us questions and let us tell him about Eddie.

Eddie had helped us discover things about ourselves. First that we are all mortal. Second, that even in the depths of mourning, some things can make you laugh. Rich recounted that because he was not a good swimmer, he could not help to save Eddie, and when the two boys were in the water, he had felt like Tarzan's pet chimpanzee, Cheeta, hopping and jumping around on the bank while Tarzan was saving Jane

The *Quarry Pond*

from the crocodiles.

And Eddie's sister Cannie had claimed that Eddie had not really drowned, but had died of shock. She said that once when the rescue squad was administering artificial respiration, Eddie sat up, looked the guy right in the eye, and then laid back and died. We didn't believe it. After more than an hour underwater, we figured he had drowned. Jack, who had come dangerously close, told us that drowning would be a quick and relatively painless way to go. We took his word for it.

For days after the accident, my friends and I sat around not feeling much joy, thinking about Eddie and the permanence of death. It was the only September I can remember that I welcomed the beginning of school, the seventh grade.

But deep inside I harbored one selfish and nagging fear. That was that my parents, in their efforts to protect me from downing, might never let me fish again. But that fear was unfounded. They explained that one difference between me and Eddie was that I could swim and Eddie could not. And my father, once an able-bodied seaman on a Great Lakes ore carrier, knew that the pleasure of existing near water carries with it the risk of drowning.

The next spring, when opening day of trout season approached, my desire to fish had come back. But none of us who knew Eddie Babich ever fished again

Fishing with My Uncles

in the Quarry Pond. And even now, half a century later, I cannot drive past the quarry, which is now surrounded by condominiums, without imagining the last gasps of the short and tragic life of Eddie Babich, and Jack Parent's heroic efforts to save him.

Hiking at Night in Underwear

❦

In August 1947, Mutt and Loo invited me to fish with them one afternoon way up on the Big Onion. My grandmother had made three pasties. A pasty—rhymes with nasty—is a popular Upper Peninsula meal made by enclosing chopped meat, potatoes, onions and sometimes rutabagas in a pie crust and baking it. (Cornish people who immigrated to the Upper Peninsula to work in the mines brought these to America. Pasties remain warm after several hours.) On our way out of town we stopped and Loo bought some soda pop, before he piloted his black Anglia up the Big Bay Road. The plan was to fish until 6 p.m. then return in early evening to Mutt's tiny trailer. He had temporarily parked it at Hawk's Nest on state land, while he and his wife, Violet, looked for a place to live.

Past the Little Onion we turned off the gravel and onto a two-track road. We drove across rusty culverts with holes in the tops, through deep puddles, over branches of trees downed in a windstorm sometime in the past year, and straddled two-foot-deep tire ruts. I think we were at least three miles in from the Big Bay Road by the time they decided that we had gone far enough. Mutt pulled the car off what was left of the road into an opening in the woods barely wide enough to fit the car into without opening the doors. We crawled out the windows with our tackle and headed in a direction that Mutt and Loo had decided on by compromise after some discussion as to which way the stretch of the Big Onion they had in mind lay. We left the pasties and pop in the car as we figured we'd be back for a late supper in a couple of hours.

When we were 10 minutes from the car, the sky

Hiking at Night in Underwear

darkened. In five more minutes there was lightning and thunder. In three more minutes we were soaked through and through. We plodded on. The underbrush was dense, and in many places you could not see your feet, nor could you see downed limbs concealed beneath the bracken ferns, joe-pye weeds, thistles and bedstraw. Every so often, at unpredictable intervals, my shin would encounter a stout limb and I would lurch forward, sometimes falling to the muddy ground and sometimes staying upright by running a few steps to get my legs back beneath my body. The situation of running a few steps and suddenly encountering another hidden alder stem among the weeds would enhance the misery as it would remove a small bit of skin from the front of my shin as I fell, hands first, onto the muddy ground among the lush August vegetation. But resting was not a good idea. Thousands of mosquitoes programmed to follow the carbon dioxide gradient to its source—my skin—would zero in within seconds.

So we plodded and stumbled on looking for this secret spot on a wonderful trout stream—a place known only to Mutt and Loo, and not all that well by them, apparently.

An hour after we left the car we had still not found a stream. Loo and Mutt then agreed on a new direction, but by now the sun was obscured by large cumulus clouds. I think we headed south, or maybe east. By

Fishing with My Uncles

about 8 p.m. (just guessing on both counts as neither watch nor compass was regarded as acceptable equipment) we finally came across a stream large enough for a trout to swim in. We fished downstream for an hour, and caught no fish, and just before dark, came out at the Big Bay Road, a revolting development for two reasons. First, we had been fishing the Little Onion, not the Big Onion, in a place where dozens of people had already fished during the season (although we saw none of them) and second, we were probably three miles from the car and the pasties, and it was now nearly dark. The good points were that we knew where we were and it had stopped raining.

A short way along the woods road toward the car, Mutt and Loo figured there was no point in all three of us walking in, so they left me by one of the rickety bridges over a puddle. I was hungry, and now it was dark. I waited and waited.

How long does it take for two men to walk three miles and then drive three miles on a rough road? Maybe two hours? How long has it been? There was no moon, but the sky had cleared and the stars were out. A few frogs near a puddle made noises and plopped about. The mosquitoes were almost intolerable. I waited, pacing up and down the road (a moving target is not quite as vulnerable to biting insects as a stationary one). Perhaps three hours later I heard voices. Mutt and Loo were approaching on foot. They

Hiking at Night in Underwear

handed me a pasty and a six-ounce brown corrugated bottle of Orange Crush, and tried to explain why they couldn't drive the car, and that we now had to walk. In their efforts to turn the car around they had broken a tie rod, making steering impossible. I sat down and ate the delicious pasty and swigged the delicious but scant Orange Crush.

Then we set out for Mutt's temporary encampment, a small trailer, at Hawk's Nest, about 4 miles back south down the Big Bay Road. Mutt and Loo's wet pants were binding their legs, so they took them off and carried them. A few cars passed us headed north. I wondered what the occupants of those cars thought when their headlights revealed three pedestrians, two men in their shirts and underpants walking purposely down the road at midnight, and one boy about 100 yards behind them, pretending he did not know the guys ahead. I felt lucky that no cars came south. I did not want to be picked up under those circumstances. But who would have picked us up, anyhow?

At about 1 a.m. we strolled into Mutt's encampment. Loo's wife, Ruth, Mutt's wife, Violet, and my mother were there enjoying the night, sitting by a fire, eating popcorn and planning tomorrow's search for us. We told them about the day's adventures and misadventures to their great amusement. At one point Ruth asked, "Mutt, are you planning to join a nudist colony?"

"Why's that?" he asked.

"You don't have your pants on."

"Oh Jeez," he said, and quickly disappeared into his trailer.

The next day, Mutt and Loo drove back up and into the woods with a few wrenches and a new tie rod and rescued the Anglia. I had found something else to do.

Uncle Clarence, Frolings' Farm, and the Wilsons

❧

In 1940, when I was seven years old, our family of four moved into a new small house on the east side of Marquette, only a quarter mile from the Lake Superior beach. I made friends with several kids around my age who lived within a couple of blocks of our house. Among these were two Wilson families, one being those of Martin Wilson, who had married Clara Peterson, and the other, Lowell Wilson, who was Martin's brother, married to Abby Froling, who was Clara's cousin. They had all been brought up in a farming area, southeast of Marquette, but now lived in town.

Martin and Lowell both worked as skilled laborers at the Lake Shore Engineering Company, which at that time was manufacturing various equipment for mines and for the shipping industry. The Lowell Wilsons had a son, Bob, two years older than I, and three lovely daughters, Ruth, Joyce and Helen. The Martin Wilson children consisted of Charlie, two years younger than I, Paul, three years younger than I, and

Fishing with My Uncles

Dorothy, a couple of years younger than Paul.

Shortly after moving into the neighborhood I learned that the Wilsons (both families) had separate properties on the Chalk River, about 15 miles southeast of town. I also found out that if I hung around with either of the families, I would be invited to go with them when they visited these properties, which was practically every Sunday. This was especially true if I attended Sunday school at the Grace Methodist Church.

I remember fondly climbing into the back seat of the Martin Wilsons' Model-A Ford cramped in with three other kids and their cocker spaniel, Roger, to visit their new property at the junction of the Chalk River and Thomson's Creek. Sometimes I would be invited by the Lowell Wilsons to the Frolings' farm, which was still producing potatoes and corn, and milk from a few cows. Froling's farm house was a thing of wonder to me. It was two stories tall, and it had been constructed of squared logs with concrete between them to seal the cracks. There was a barn for the cattle and for storing hay. The Chalk River meandered through the property, first flowing north, then turning to the east. About an acre of land bordered on two sides by the river was used as a garden, and a majestic clump of elms, called by the family "The Twelve Apostles," was the centerpiece. Unfortunately, the Apostles began to pass away with old age and Dutch

Uncle Clarence, Frolings' Farm, and the Wilsons

Elm disease until all were gone. Bob Wilson and I would fish the stream, and nearly invariably would be able to take enough brook and rainbow trout for a meal.

Clarence Froling had been the last one to occupy the house permanently, his three sisters being occupied elsewhere, although once in a while they would show up at their former home.

One evening, the women (aunts and mothers) set up a card table and proceeded to ask the table questions that could be answered "yes" or "no." The table would, according to them, respond by knocking one of its legs on the floor, one knock for "no" and two knocks for "yes." They would ask such questions as whether Bob would catch any fish the following day, or whether Joyce (one of Bob's older sisters) would get a job soon, etc. The most stunning one, however, was, "Will Clarence get married within the next few months?" The table answered with two knocks.

There were lots of giggles, and Bob and I were stunned. Clarence was nearly 50 years old and never showed any signs of wanting to get married. Clarence had been our friend and chaperone, as our parents always wanted an adult to be present at the farm when we were there.

"What does a table know about Clarence's love life?" we asked ourselves. Was our bachelor fishing companion possibly deserting us for marriage? Bob

Fishing with My Uncles

and I could not believe it.

About two months later, Clarence married a divorcée, Edna DeSautelle, who was a lovely lady, and she and Clarence lived at the farm for a few years, as Clarence commuted to his job in town.

When Bob and I were in high school we often stayed for a few days in the summer, mostly fishing. In the late 1940s, the Michigan Conservation Department (now called the Department of Natural Resources) made a practice of stocking brook trout in suitable lakes and streams. Once, when Bob and I were staying at the farm for a few days, Clarence heard some commotion downstream a few hundred yards from the house.

He investigated and found that a truck from the Michigan Conservation Department had bogged down in a mud hole in the two-rut road next to the river. The truck was carrying a load of legal-sized (7 to 9 inches long), hatchery-reared brook trout. They had been distributing them along the river, but still had lots of fish left in the tank. The only way to get the truck out of the mudhole was to empty its load of water, and maybe 1,000 or more naive trout, in one place in the Chalk River.

They did so and drove away. Clarence told Bob and me that we should go fishing and that there were a lot of fish to be caught about 200 yards from the house. We both went down to the site of the truck

Uncle Clarence, Frolings' Farm, and the Wilsons

mishap, and found that recently stocked brook trout are hungry and gullible. We each took our legal limit of 15. It was not even fun after catching the first four or five.

But Clarence, who had experienced the poverty of the Great Depression, and who had recently purchased a deep freeze, was unable to pass up this opportunity. As I recall, he, and perhaps his recent bride, made about three trips to the scene of the sudden trout population explosion, and filled a goodly part of the freezer.

About a half mile downstream from the Frolings' farm, the Martin Wilson family bought property and constructed a substantial home. The Martin Wilsons were as generous as the Frolings, and we had many years fishing the Chalk and Olson Creek. We never caught very many fish, but I recall one special day in which Charlie, Paul and I each caught perhaps three good-sized trout, 7 to 10 inches long on the Olson (not stocked, judging from their color). We promptly named the place "Fishermen's Paradise," although it never again quite lived up to that name.

On extra-special summer days, the senior Wilson brothers, Lowell and Martin, occasionally took us kids to their boyhood home, about 10 miles away through the woods from the Chalk properties. The vacant but still stately house was surrounded by grassy hillsides, and a path to a lake named for their family beckoned

Fishing with My Uncles

us. We often picked blueberries or raspberries, but mainly I recall catching smallmouth bass in the lake. We did so by stirring up the water as we swam in it. Then sometimes we would bait our hooks with grasshoppers, cast them out and let them sink to the bottom. Apparently the bass did not ask the question as to how a grasshopper managed to get to the bottom of the lake, but it must have looked good to eat. We would catch a few bass, and they themselves looked good to eat, and they were. Visiting Wilson Lake always seemed to be a special treat, perhaps epitomizing the height of summer, family and friendship.

Religion and Trout Fishing

☜

My devotion to the Methodist faith began to wane when I was about 14 years old. I think the turning point was one Easter Sunday when some of us Sunday School students stayed for the regular service and the sermon, in my case perhaps to find some message in the Resurrection that could be applied to catching fish. The Bible was a bit shy on that subject, although the story of the loaves and the fishes did catch my attention.

Reverend Eglund, noting a fair number of young people in the congregation, was pleased with our interest and decided to give us a few words about Easter. He said that if you get up before dawn on Easter morning and watch the sun come up it "dances on the horizon" as a celebration of the ascension of Christ.

By that time, I had had some science in school. In order for the sun to appear to "dance" on the horizon, either the sun had to do some gyrations in its position in space relative to the earth, or an illusion of a dancing sun could be created by the earth jerking back and forth in its rotation on its axis. And, if that would happen for every kid who was watching, all around the world, the earth would have to be jerking

Fishing with My Uncles

back and forth all Easter day, as it is always dawn somewhere on this planet, especially near the equinox. I figured that, if true, this phenomenon would have been reported somewhere besides in the Grace Methodist Church in Marquette. As far as I was concerned, Reverend Eglund's credibility was pretty well shot. It was only two weeks before trout season opened. As the sermon droned on, I day-dreamed a brook trout ascending to my Royal Coachman.

My faith in the church was gone, but the Wilsons, who nearly always invited me to church with them, continued to generously share their meals, invitations to fish, and kindness to me and to all others. For me that was the most tangible and valuable feature of Christianity, and these traits were epitomized by the Wilsons and the Frolings.

Fishing with Ernest Hemingway

❦

In 1947 my mother was reading Ernest Hemingway. Among his classics, including *For Whom the Bell Tolls*, *The Sun also Rises*, and *A Farewell to Arms*, was a story called "The Big Two-Hearted River."

My mother brought it to me and said, "Read this story. I think you'll enjoy it."

It was an absorbing tale, especially for a trout fisherman. Through his alter ego, Nick Adams, Hemingway describes a solitary pilgrimage, beginning when he gets off the train in the fire-ravaged village of Seney, in the eastern Upper Peninsula, about 90 miles from Marquette. After the train pulls away, Nick walks a short distance to where a stream flows under a trestle. He sees some trout fanning in the current, a few of them large. He is pleased.

But he does not fish here, near the town. Memories of horrors recently witnessed in Europe in the war of 1917-18 creep into his consciousness. He shoulders his pack and heads northeast, at first on a road, then on trails. He sees the ridges separating the streams that flow toward Lake Michigan from those

Fishing with My Uncles

flowing northward to Lake Superior. As he walks, the images of war become more remote.

Once he stops to pluck some leaves of sweet fern, crushes them and puts them beneath the shoulder of his pack, so that he can enjoy their fragrance as he walks. The farther he goes, the less are the effects of the fires. He enters a forest, pitches his tent and eats a mixture of a can of spaghetti and a can of baked beans. He sleeps the night near the stream, in a peacefulness he had not experienced in years. The next day he catches several trout, using grasshoppers for bait, and keeps two of the larger fish to eat.

Hemingway had described something deeper about fishing than simply catching fish, something that even at the age of 14 I could understand.

"Did you like the story?" my mother asked.

"Yes, I did," I was an ardent reader of fishing stories in outdoor magazines, but this was nothing like those.

"We have to go there," my mother said. I agreed.

We found the Two-Hearted River on the road map, and a few days later we packed the black humpbacked 1937 Ford with one brown canvas umbrella tent, assorted pots and pans, boots, father, mother, my 9-year-old brother Dick, me, and an 8-week-old cocker spaniel with white feet.

By 4 p.m., after a dusty ride, over many miles of gravel roads, we found the river. We were now some

20 miles in a straight line northeast of Seney. Here there was a steel bridge across the Two-Hearted and a state forest campground nearby. Seven or eight other camping parties had campfires going and tents pitched near their cars. Our supposed sacred river had been invaded by picnic tables, a gravel driveway and tent sites. The dense forest that Hemingway had described had been cleared and the ground flattened. At 5 p.m. we heard a factory whistle blow, not a half-mile from us. We learned the next day that it was from a blueberry-canning factory.

We fished the Two-Hearted River and caught a few small trout. They were not the noble native brook trout, but rainbows, several generations removed from rainbow trout from the Pacific Coast, stocked 50 years earlier in the Great Lakes by fish managers attempting to improve the fishing. We followed the river upstream some distance, and caught no brook trout. We began to suspect that Hemingway had used his poetic license rather freely.

Hemingway never claimed that any of his stories were literally true. But somehow we thought that this one should have been, because it took place in the Upper Peninsula and he used the name of a real town and a real river. The people at the campground were not there to fish, it seemed, and they appeared oblivious of Hemingway's pilgrimage about three decades earlier. They did not seem to share my mother's and

Fishing with My Uncles

my view that this river should have been a sacred place, sanctified by the words of our new spiritual leader, Ernest Hemingway. But Hemingway was a writer of fiction. He no more claimed truth in "The Big Two-Hearted River," than in "The Snows of Kilimanjaro" or *A Farewell to Arms*.

In the late 1950s, about 10 years after the Robinson Voyage to the blueberry cannery on the Two-Hearted River, Dr. Sheridan Baker, Professor of English at the University of Michigan, also attempted to retrace Hemingway's footsteps in the story. Dr. Baker was teaching summer school at Northern Michigan University in Marquette and took this opportunity to visit Seney, and hike from there to the Two-Hearted River, following the directions poetically described in the story.

He discovered that the stream that passes beneath the railroad tressle is the West Branch of the Fox. He, as our family did in 1947, found that it would have been impossible to hike with full backpack cross-country from Seney to the Two-Hearted River in a single afternoon, in which Nick Adams included a long nap. As Baker put it, "Hemingway's River is ... not the Two-Hearted ... He simply found a symbolic title ready-made, reaching over the swamps and pines to borrow a name closer to his meaning than the [river he fished] could provide."

Many of us who fish for trout in relatively small

streams are reluctant to disclose the names of streams when we find good fishing, because the numbers of fish in small streams are finite, trout are fun to catch, they are good to eat and many people seek them for those reasons. Trout streams can be fished out rather quickly. In addition, searching for and finding a good place to catch trout is almost as satisfying as catching the fish in them. In other words, getting out of the car, fishing in a hatchery pool and catching one trout after another has no appeal. On the other hand, finding a stream on a map, hiking over hills and through swamps and finding an isolated beaver pond or stretch of stream with good-sized native trout in it and no human footprints is the dream of most backwoods brook trout fishermen. Thus the satisfaction of fishing for brook trout involves much more than just catching fish.

What stream, then, did Hemingway fish? I will not say for fear that publicity will cause other fishermen to love it to death. But I did fish the stream once. Hemingway wrote, "Nick did not like to fish with other men on the river. Unless they were of your party, they spoiled it." Hemingway and my uncles shared that view.

In August 1968, Harry Harju, a native of Newberry, guided me on a trip to the stream that is probably the one that Hemingway fished. It had rained heavily during the night before Harry and I arrived and the water was high. At dawn as the thunder and light rain passed to the east, we launched a small boat with a small motor. We traveled upstream and once the motor struck a log and Harry had to replace the shear pin, and we pulled ashore. I tied on a Mickey Finn streamer fly. The water was high and slightly cloudy from the rain. I had little hope of getting a trout to rise to the surface because abundant food was probably riding the currents in the depths and a trout would not need to come to the surface to obtain food. But I could try a few casts while Harry did the motor mechanics. On my second cast, however, a large fish took the fly. I thought maybe 15 or 16 inches. But as I played the fish it made one pass beside the grounded boat, and I saw it was considerably larger. "Woho," I said. "That's a big fish," and my heart rate doubled. After 10 minutes the fish tired and I led it into Harry's landing net. It was a brown trout, 24 inches long, weighing 4-1/2 pounds, the largest trout that I have ever caught on a fly. Its silvery appearance indicated that it had probably spent most of its life in one of the Great Lakes and was now ascending the stream to spawn. Brown trout, and rainbow, were introduced into Michigan waters. It was not the preferred species, but this one was a beautiful fish. We went on to catch some smaller but respectable brook trout later that morning. We saw no other fishermen. Hemingway's stream still has brook trout in it, and if

Fishing with Ernest Hemingway

one approaches it cross-country, solitude can still be found. Seney has fewer people in it now than in the 1920s, and you may fish his stream all day and not see another person. Hemingway might be pleased.

A Trout Stream, A Man and Two Boys

❧

One day in late July, Loo took Jack Parent and me way up on the Little Onion. Loo and Mutt always fished "way up" on every stream. To do less would risk seeing another fisherman. Jack and I were about 13 and 14 years old.

We left the black Anglia not far off the main road and hiked a couple of miles westward up the Silver Mine Road. Then we headed south, cross-country through the woods toward the stream. By late July, the mosquitoes have pretty well had their day, laid their eggs and died, making fishing more pleasant. After a short distance, we broke out of the forest suddenly onto a rock outcrop about 25 feet above a beaver meadow. The scene before us was unforgettable.

Beneath a blue nearly cloudless sky the stream, 10 to 15 feet wide, wound among clumps of alders through a meadow created by centuries of beavers building dams then abandoning them as food became scarce, building dams again several years later when the alders had recovered, and so on. Patches of Joe-pye-weed held their lavender flowers to the sun, hum-

A Trout Stream, A Man and Two Boys

mocks of grasses and sedges swayed in a gentle summer wind and the repeated song of a veery came from the maples on the hillside we had just left. The stream flowed toward us into a small pool, about three feet deep just beneath where we had emerged from the woods. Near the head of the pool to the right of the main current we could see a 6-inch brook trout, his size magnified both by the water and our imaginations. His black, orange and white pectoral fins gave away his otherwise nearly perfect camouflage of brown and black mottling on his back. The multicolored bottom of the stream reflected sunlight, which also sparkled from the surface of the water. The stream flowed to our left, over a submerged log, then down through a gravel riffle, disappearing among the tall grasses and alders. As we started down the rocks, the small trout we had watched darted upstream and disappeared beneath the stream bank.

We worked our way down to the stream. Once we were into the shade of the alders, Loo began to dig worms with a stick. I was old enough now to appreciate the humanity of this kind and gentle man: Richard Lewis Robinson, the youngest of the three brothers. This was a man small in stature who could sit at a pipe organ and set the mood of the Episcopal congregation from one of private meditation and humility to one of triumph and joy. He could also fill his basement, and occasionally the neighborhood, with Bach

Fishing with My Uncles

fugues played *fortissimo* from his own pipe organ that he had purchased and installed.

I looked now at his delicate, graceful and talented hands so beautifully trained, as he grasped an escaping earthworm. There was dirt beneath his nails and in every wrinkle of the skin of his hands. Are these the same hands, I asked myself, now grubbing into the fragrant black soil, his fingers dappled with the slime of worms, that will, in a few days produce sounds so beautiful in the church that it will make one almost believe the words that are said in such an atmosphere?

As I contemplated this relationship between the beauty of nature, music and religion, and my uncle's role in this triangle, Loo grabbed quickly at a big worm. "Ah ha! I gotcha!" he said and put it into his tobacco can with several others.

We fished for a while and all three of us caught a few trout. In mid-afternoon it became downright hot. We came to a beaver pond where the water was five feet deep. We took off our clothes (leaving our underpants on for modesty) and swam for several minutes.

Then we dressed and continued down the stream sometimes separated by more than 100 yards and sometimes coming together to talk about fish that got away, and the few that we kept.

How many fish did we catch that day, and how big were they? I do not remember, nor do I remember catching any big ones (over 10 inches long), which probably means we didn't. We walked out of the woods in the fading daylight of this summer day, got into the Anglia and were home at dark.

This was not a day when we filled our creels with fish, nor one in which very exciting things happened. Jack Parent and I are now in our early 70s. We don't see each other often, but a few years ago Jack and I were talking. We had not mentioned that fishing trip for 50 years. Jack brought up the day that Loo took us both fishing. And we both remember it almost exactly as I have described it here. It was not the fish that made the day, but it was a special communion between a trout stream, two boys and a very kind and talented man.

Fishing with My Mother

❦

We were on the Black Cat one bright day in July. Here among the sandy plains, the Cat runs mostly slowly over a sandy bottom where alders reach out across it, nearly touching in the middle. It was just my mother and I. The trout were not biting well. At times such as this my mind wanders. I've been interested in birds most of my life, so I rarely pass up an opportunity to get a good look at a spotted sandpiper along the stream edge, a Parula warbler in the black spruce, or a black-billed cuckoo in the willows.

I looked down the stream about 30 yards and caught a glimpse of rapidly moving orange and dark blue-gray. It was something about 6 inches long and flitting about five feet above the water in the alders. It seemed to want to fly away but then would stop and be still. "Orange and blue-gray or black," I thought. "Maybe a redstart. Not the right habitat for an oriole." I kept leafing through my mental bird book and began to sneak downstream to see if I could get a closer look. I might have to look this one up in my Roger Tory Peterson. It kept fluttering in the same spot, perhaps catching small insects in the alders, I thought.

Then slowly from beneath I saw a human hand reach up to the struggling animal. It was my mother's hand. The "bird" was a brook trout in a tree.

"How did a fish get up in a tree?" I wondered. After fishing with my mother since I was very young, I should have known.

My mother's favorite kind of fishing was in small trout streams, using a worm for bait. The approved method of catching a trout in such an environment is to gently lower a baited hook with a small split shot sinker a few inches above the hook, into a hole under the bank or below a log. Upon getting a bite you give the line a little slack to let the fish get the hook fully into its mouth, then you give a short, sharp jerk, moving the rod tip perhaps six inches to a foot, to set the hook into the fish's mouth. Then you slowly retrieve the struggling trout, eventually lifting it in a gentle arc

Fishing with My Uncles

Step 2

into your hand if the fish is small (under nine inches); if it is larger, you usually retrieve the fish by keeping it in the water at all times, and eventually clasp it behind its gills with one hand or head it into a landing net. The result is a satisfying and somewhat ritual experience that may last for 10 to 30 seconds, and allows one to form memorable mental images of the pleasure of fishing.

My mother did not subscribe to that technique. When a fish bit, she would respond immediately by yanking as hard as she could. Her approach was a brief two-step process. First, get the fish airborne as quickly as possible, and second, grab the fish from wherever it happens to stop. Sometimes this would be on the ground 12 feet behind her, but often it would be in a tree somewhere over her head.

I have never fished with anyone who would get as excited about catching a trout as my mother. Any trout longer than seven inches on her line would gen-

Step 3

erate a flow of adrenaline equivalent to that of a baseball player hitting a home run with the bases loaded to win the World Series. Her hands would tremble and she could hardly get the hook from the fish's mouth.

I believe the last trout she ever caught was also the biggest. It was a rainbow, 23 inches long. She had taken my father, who had had a stroke and was no longer able to fish, for a drive one day in late May and they stopped near the railroad bridge on Wallace Creek. She baited up with a worm and looked beneath the bridge and saw this fine trout fanning in the current. Her worm hit the water. The trout hit the worm, and two seconds later the trout was flopping on the gravel in the middle of the road behind her. No fuss, no muss, no ceremony, just a little sand and gravel to wash off in the sink at home. But her trembling hands made it hard to keep the car on the road for the 15-mile trip back to town.

The Summer of '51

At 7:25 a.m. June 16, 1951, I walked across the railroad tracks and through the gate into the Cliffs-Dow Chemical Plant's grounds. I heard a familiar voice behind me. "Billy," it said, "You working here too?" I turned around. It was Mutt.

"Yep," I answered with little enthusiasm. "What are you doing here?"

"Going to work," Mutt chuckled. "I'm starting today, too. You know, it was exactly 25 years ago when I started to work here the first time. I stayed less than a year. Couldn't take it." He chuckled again.

Loo had been at the gate when we checked in. He had been working there several years already, mostly sitting in the gate house, recording punch-in and punch-out times, calculating hours worked, and making sure everyone punched only his own card so that no one could escape over the fence and have someone else punch out for him. He had chuckled and offered some friendly words as I had passed his portal. Beyond the gate Mutt and I blended in among the college boys and temporarily reformed derelicts who had responded to the recent ad in the newspaper announcing the hiring of 40 men. We all trudged

The Summer of '51

through the morning haze around a dirty brick building to meet our bosses. So for a short while in the summer of 1951 my two fraternal uncles and I worked at the same place.

The air at the plant always smelled—bad. In Marquette you could tell when the wind shifted to the north because the smell would tell you. The work was horrible—digging chemical sludge from trenches, loading bags of black dusty charcoal onto trucks, scraping and painting eight-inch beams supporting a vertical retort 80 feet above the ground with no safety devices, and cleaning acid scum from inside a huge fractionating column.

For the latter job, done only about twice a year to minimize down-time, about 20 of us worked from 6 a.m. until after midnight. The bosses told us to wear old clothes for that day.

The job entailed squeezing through tight manholes in a vertical retort, with an electric light on a cord, unscrewing some perforated steel cups, and tossing the cups, which weighed a couple of pounds, down to other crew members on the floor, where they would clean and brush the scum from them in solvents and pass them back up. If a catcher missed a cup it could land on his foot or hit his knee and it would hurt. At the end of the day we each got $3.75 cash, on top of our $1.12 an hour, to pay for clothes, which by evening were literally eaten away by the chemicals

Fishing with My Uncles

we contacted while cleaning the cups and shelves.

Working along with us that day was a man in his 30s who communicated frequently with God. Tall and gaunt, he would, I had heard from my friends who worked closely with him, pause occasionally during the day and get down on one knee to seek solace or to give thanks. Solace was by far the more common motive in that place. About 2 p.m. all our muscles were aching and our skin itched and burned. This gentleman, who had been catching and cleaning cups and was not a very good catcher, knelt for a short visit with God. He got up and said, "The Lord doesn't want me to work here anymore," and headed for the gate. We never saw him again. As it turns out he was probably smarter than all the rest of us. We left at midnight and reported at 7:30 the next morning.

In 1968 the plant closed, leaving a legacy of toxic waste, some of which Mutt and I had shoveled by hand, without masks or protective clothing. In the 1980s the abandoned plant site was declared by the U.S. Environmental Protection Agency as a Superfund Cleanup Site. In the winter of 1993-94, 10 acres of chemical sludge were dug up by men in space suits with gas masks, loaded into tightly enclosed and secured rail cars and shipped to a toxic waste incinerator in the southwestern United States.

I quit at Cliffs-Dow in mid-August 1951, when I had enough money for next year's tuition. Mutt had already left. A few days after I quit, Mutt, Loo and I fished way up on the Onion. We let the rain and the stream wash the chemicals from our skin and replaced them with the clear, pure slime of earthworms and brook trout, and felt the moist black earth beneath our fingernails.

Loo, who had worked at Cliffs-Dow for 25 years, died of throat cancer in 1968 at age 64. His father had lived to be 78, his mother 92. His two brothers, Tom and Mutt, lived into their 80s.

Good Things Must End

֍

I never telephoned my uncle Loo and he never called me. There were two reasons for this. For most of the time, he lived across the street from me, and he hated the telephone.

The proper way to communicate with him would be either to visit him or write him a letter. The middle ground, a telephone call, was simply too rude and demanding. A ring, he has to get up and pick the thing up; if he doesn't, it keeps ringing in an irritating way. If he answers it, there's a nasal replica of the caller's voice, or it is a wrong number. And he can't look eye-to-eye with the caller. Loo often worked the midnight shift at the plant and tried to sleep during the day. Of course the telephone would ring during the day, for his wife, Ruth, or for one of the three kids. Loo would hear it ring. "The world's worst invention," he would say.

About two months before the throat cancer got him, Lake Superior had frozen smoothly one night. Usually in fall and winter Lake Superior is at its wildest off Marquette, churned by the wind. Smooth ice, as one usually imagines the winter surface of a lake, seldom forms. Waves heave surface ice into small chunks and throw them against the shore. Other

Good Things Must End

waves follow, and huge dunes of ice form as water splashes up and freezes up to 15 feet high with caves and spouts like geysers. But in Loo's last winter as he fought the cancer, one windless night the lake froze as smoothly as a skating rink. The next day, Loo rummaged about the house and found an old pair of ice skates that fit him. He drove to the Lower Harbor and put his skates on at the cinder pond. He swiftly glided out around the breakwater and turned north gliding and striding, long smooth strokes across the bluish clear ice, a tiny solitary figure on the largest surface of fresh water ice in the world. He went beyond Picnic Rocks like magic in the bright sunshine, alone, breathing with some difficulty. Then after another half-mile he turned, heading back to the south. To his right now were the shore, the pines, the ice dunes on the beach and the houses of the city. This was his home, where he was born, and where he had played such beautiful music. Fifteen minutes later, he glided around the end of the breakwater, and into the harbor. He took his skates off and got into his little pickup truck, a luxury of his brief retirement, and drove home. He told me about it the next day.

Just before trout season opened (and a month before Decoration Day, Loo's unofficial start of fishing season), Loo entered St. Mary's Hospital. About 10 days later he died. After his funeral I fished by myself. It was a windy, dry day in early May. The new

Fishing with My Uncles

leaves had not emerged and last year's brown ones were blowing about and covering much of the water. There was no other fisherman. I caught one eight-inch brook trout and kept it. Loo would have done so. It was nearly dark when I left, talking with my uncle's spirit. I could not help thinking of his description of the one time he fished on the last day of the season: "I didn't enjoy it. Fished all day with a lump in my throat."

The Disabled Veteran

🐢

While fishing the Chalk River late one August afternoon, I came upon a turtle in a patch of sunshine on a sandy strip between the water and the alders. At first he tried to escape me by hobbling toward the stream, but when he realized he could not make it before I reached him, he stopped and went into his turtle defense posture—legs and head tucked almost entirely into his shell. I had not seen a turtle such as this before. He was neither a painted nor snapping turtle, which are by far the most common turtles in the reptile-unfriendly climate of the Upper Peninsula. He was bigger than most painted turtles, but smaller than most snapping turtles.

I picked him up to examine him more closely. His carapace was bumpy, and his belly armor was yellow and decorated with inky blotches. Rings on his scales told me he was old. He urinated without emotion or shame. Later that evening I looked him up in a book. Humans have named his kind "Blanding's turtle." Neither the turtle nor I knew who Blanding was.

His left hind leg was totally missing with skin long ago grown over its socket. His right hand was also missing, but the two forearm bones protruded outward from healed-over skin. "Captain Hook," I thought, and wondered what tales of battles this veteran could tell, if we could communicate more clearly. After a few minutes his head came out, almost asking, "How long is this going to take?"

So I set him down and watched him limp into a quiet part of a pool. He sank about two feet to the bottom and was still. But now he was watching me. I sat down on a nearby log and ate a packaged cake baked the day before in Minneapolis and drank a soft drink from an aluminum pop-top can with bright paint on it. The turtle remained motionless.

I felt him telling me about turtles. His kind had seen the earth once as steaming subtropical swamps and mild uplands in which the reptiles—dinosaurs, lizards, alligators, snakes, and yes, modestly, to some extent, turtles dominated the fauna. Through the centuries his kind had seen the mountains rise and temperatures drop, causing thousands of reptiles to perish gradually. Meanwhile, the birds, once reptiles themselves, but now with their constant body temperature and feathers for warmth and flight, could fly great distances to escape the winters. And the mammals, with large brains, and fur to protect them from the cold, were taking over, especially in areas far from the equator. These upstarts out-survived and out-bred the reptiles. Only the insects among the animals seemed more abundant.

The veteran reminded me that he had won that

The Disabled Veteran

silly race with the hare, and, all in all, the turtles had done well. But now with fewer and fewer streams and quiet ponds to inhabit, these young upstarts, humans, which I was born a member of, with our chemicals, our consuming of forests and our damming of his streams, were putting him to yet another test. And he was old and tired.

I got up to leave. The veteran, still quiet in the tea-colored water, remained. I felt him watching me, probably with some relief, as I disappeared downstream around the bend with my fancy fishing tackle.

Farewell to the Rebel

❦

The last time I saw Mutt was in the intensive care unit in Marquette General Hospital. It was the second Sunday in May—Mother's Day, 1984. His eyes brightened when he saw me, and he smiled. He was 82 years old, sitting up with tubes through his mouth and nose.

"Mutt," I said, "You look like a carburetor."

He smiled some more. It was his kind of joke. He couldn't talk. He had survived Hodgkins disease in the early 1970s and had been healthy since then, doing carpentry work, maintaining his house and writing a book. I asked him how the maple sugaring had gone this spring. He nodded his head, then tried to say something, his eyebrows raised. It sounded like "Ooh ah uh?"

I think he was asking "You want some?" but I wasn't sure, and I didn't want to repeat it for fear he wasn't really offering it.

The funeral was three days later. On a simple table was a brass urn with the remains and beside it a photograph of Henry M. Robinson, Chief Petty Officer, United States Navy. He looked proud and handsome, wearing a small mustache and his officer's cap. The

Farewell to the Rebel

minister who said the words did not know Mutt, which was not surprising, as Mutt had not spent more than a few hours in church in his life and did not consort with the clergy. At this time he had no power to stop this man from saying things that would embarrass him. He would have laughed at the poor guy trying to find good and consoling things to say to the small gathering of friends and relatives.

I think of Mutt each time I wade too deep and water pours into my hip boots (useless things!) and when darkness comes, and I'm still a mile from the car and don't know exactly which way it is, and it's starting to rain.

Fishing with My Uncles

A Day with the Master

❧

John Voelker, alias Robert Traver, is a U.P. legend: lawyer, prosecuting attorney, Justice of the Michigan Supreme Court, author of *Anatomy of a Murder, Trout Magic, Trout Madness, Small Town D.A.* and other contemplative and adventurous books about the Upper Peninsula. In the movie version of *Anatomy of a Murder*, Voelker was played by James Stewart, and they had become friends.

John showed up to meet me at the Crossroads on a Sunday in September 1981, driving his Subaru Brat, right on time. He was 78 years old. I had met him two nights earlier at the Crow's Nest, a restaurant high atop a hotel in Marquette. When my wife and I arrived, John was sitting at the piano playing "As Time Goes By," and playing it quite well. Near the piano, two attractive young women in their 20s listened, admiring. After the introductions by Ted Bogdan, the hotel manager, John asked if we thought the two pretty young ladies appreciated his playing.

"It sure looked as if they were, John," I said, without lying. I was appreciating his playing as well.

He seemed pleased that at age 78, he could still charm young women.

When John learned that my father was Tom

Robinson, he was delighted. He began to praise my father, remembering him from high school as a wonderful trombone player who had his own jazz band. He also was pleased that I'm a U.P. native.

He had read of some of my environmental ideas and liked them. He was looking for people such as I, who might be encouraged to help to protect the Upper Peninsula from the ravages of civilization. We decided to meet the following Sunday at the Crossroads at 10 a.m. I was flattered that he would trust me with his ideas.

On this Sunday morning he wanted to show me something in the woods. We drove on roads that became fainter and fainter. Finally we stopped in an average looking part of the woods, with aspens, young maples and some balsam fir. Here was the mystery structure that John wanted to show me. It was an arrangement of now moss-covered rocks, in two parallel rows about seven feet long, two feet high, with a trough between them about a foot-and-a-half wide. At the upper end was a circular rock "chimney." Sometime earlier he had taken a university anthropologist to the site, and she had told him that it was probably a still built in the 1920s to produce moonshine.

He wasn't convinced. He wanted it to be Indian. Maybe something for making maple syrup or roasting deer, he thought. Two nights before, at the lounge,

Fishing with My Uncles

Ted Bogdan had taken me aside and said, "John wants it to be Indian— everyone he takes there thinks it was built about 50 years ago—but he's such a romantic, he won't accept that."

I couldn't help him. Anthropology was not my field. I looked around the site but found nothing—no pieces of glass or metal, and no rectangular building remnant to suggest some white man's failed attempt at something. Nor could we find circular structures to suggest aboriginal building. I remained non-committal.

John did not want the newspapers to know about it, afraid that "in two days," he said, "They'd have a popcorn stand set up and sell tickets for admission."

He had trusted me with his discovery because, as he put it, "I think you give a shit for this land." He further explained, "There are those who care and those who don't. It's as simple as that." I was flattered.

As we drove away from the mystery structure and through the woods roads, John shared some of his ideas with me. "There are three possible ways mankind will do itself in—we'll poison ourselves, we'll blow ourselves up with the bomb, or fornicate ourselves to death." He drove slowly and kept his eye out for mushrooms. (He was was an ardent mushroom hunter. It goes with trout fishing.)

"These guys in the Reagan Administration—

A Day with the Master

They're probably nice guys, not evil; they don't mean any harm, but I probably wouldn't want to have to spend much time with them. If they took these woods and paved them, I'd be foolish to argue that this is where I hunt mushrooms. They'd tell me, 'You can buy mushrooms in the store.' They wouldn't understand."

We parted shortly after noon. John was going home to watch the Green Bay Packers game on television. (Green Bay is less than 200 miles from Marquette, while Detroit is 400. Thus the Packers have more fans in this part of the Upper Peninsula than do the Lions).

I saw John Voelker several times after that but only briefly. Mostly he would be at the university library, gathering information for his writing. He'd say to me things like, "I think we should open a hunting season on logging trucks," a satirical observation on large tract clear-cutting.

John died while driving his car on a woods road a few miles from home. He had pulled over to the side and turned off the key. He died there of a heart attack, about 10 years after our visit to the mysterious ruins of Sands. It was a good way to go.

What It's All About

✒

It was not until I had nearly completed writing these stories, several years after the passing of Loo and Mutt, that I realized that they were purists. Many fly-fishermen, and fly-fisherwomen consider themselves purists, disdaining the use of live bait, such as worms and minnows, and large metallic lures.

But we should ask ourselves, how pure is using a rod made of some substance fashioned through complex technological manipulations of petroleum? Our tapered fly lines and leaders are also made from petroleum, our waders and hip boots from rubber imported from some other continent and worn to isolate us from the aquatic environment, in the interest of comfort. We use flies tied from high-tech synthetic products. Even the hackles on flies tied commercially now come from domestic roosters, bred and pampered especially for the slender hackles on their heads and necks, which increase the floatation capacity of dry flies.

 Mutt and Loo kept their relationship with trout simple and comparatively pure. Their rods and reels were made of steel, perhaps from iron mined within the county. They used lines made from cotton (a renewable resource), a few lead sinkers and simple

What It's All About

steel hooks. Their lure was nearly exclusively an earthworm, often dug with a stick from the soil near the stream in which they would fish.

They waded in cotton pants and cheap sneakers, thus fear of wading in over their boots did not exist for them. I often saw them up to their waists in deep parts of the stream. When it rained, I never saw them run for the car or put on a raincoat. For them, being wet with rain and with the water of the stream was rightfully a part of the existence of a trout fisherman.

Following is a list of equipment Mut and Loo did not use, and why:

Hip boots or waders—Too hot to walk in.

Landing net—The net gets tangled in the alders and impedes progress. So a few fish may escape; it makes for a good story.

Tackle box—If you can't carry your fishing gear in you pants pocket, you've got too much of it.

Raincoat—Too hot, especially if it isn't raining.

Compass and watch—The disdain for these two items played an important role in turning several routine fishing trips into exciting adventures, resulting in many hours of good exercise, which they would not have experienced had they known where they (and sometimes I) were and what time it was.

Trout flies—It is hard to cast a fly properly if the stream is only five feet wide and is 90 percent covered with alders.

Fishing with My Uncles

Four-wheel-drive vehicle—Too expensive, but more importantly, a good fisherman should walk at least a mile to the stream, and much more on the way back. To do less is cheating, and the easier it is to get to a stream, the more likely it is one might encounter other fishermen.

Worm container—I recall both Mutt and Loo carrying some kind of container, frequently a small metal tobacco tin that would fit into a shirt pocket. But, as I recall, they only remembered to take a tobacco can along about every other trip. This did seem to be a useful item, without which several problems arose: (1) the worms escape from your pocket, and (2) if all the worms in your pocket are not used or do not escape, they will eventually appear in the washing machine, among the other laundry items. Despite the fact that my mother was an ardent trout fisher, she did not particularly enjoy finding earthworms among the otherwise clean wash. Of course the worms did not survive their washing machine experience, which I considered a waste of good worms.

Mutt and Loo fished streams for only one species, the brook trout, one of the most beautiful of fishes, and one native to their own environment in Upper Michigan. The same environment where Mutt and Loo were born. They had little interest in catching rainbow trout (imported from streams on the West Coast of North America) nor brown trout (introduced from Europe). In fact, they avoided streams inhabited by those exotic species.

I guess there's something about eating a brook trout that they had just caught, thus becoming part of the web of life of the trout stream, and the trout becoming part of them.

Fishing with My Uncles

Last Day

↘

On September 30, 1994, I found myself, 61 years old, guiding two gentlemen on a woodcock hunt, for which they had contributed a goodly sum to the Ruffed Grouse Society. As the morning dew was slowly evaporating from the grasses and leaves of the tall asters, we were planning our strategy and trying to contain Mariah, my springer spaniel. A quarter-mile away, the Escanaba River was flowing quietly along through the final hours of the trout season. As we loaded our shotguns, a gentleman wearing a fishing vest and displaying a Trout Unlimited sticker on his car bumper passed us heading toward the river. He waved and smiled.

Envy! It was true that this was a fine day to hunt woodcock, but it was also the last day of the trout season, and a fine day to fish. It was cloudy, calm and mild. There would be insects on the surface, and trout would be feeding on them. I discovered then that Loo was only partly right, at least from my standpoint, about not enjoying the last day of trout season. You can also get a lump in your throat on the last day by *not* fishing.

We walked into the cover, Mariah bounding, tail

Last Day

wagging. For two hours, woodcock wings twittered, shotguns boomed, and sometimes a bird would fall. And there were 15-minute birdless periods, during which I found myself thinking of trout.

At lunchtime, we were back at the cars eating sandwiches. Two flocks of geese, headed south, called from high above us in the clearing sky. I suggested we walk over to the river to view its beauty as it flowed quietly among the early autumn colors. A few trout were rising. My companions were not fly fishermen. They watched the stream as they would a movie in which they could not participate or influence the outcome. I wanted badly to be a part of it.

"See that trout down there?" I asked. "That's a nice brown, about 14 inches long. I think I could catch that fish." It was feeding regularly, moving back and forth at the tail of a pool, slurping terrestrial insects.

"Do you have your tackle?" Ed asked.

"Sure. It's in my car." From May through September, I never take it out of my car except to use it. But my job today was not to fish for trout, but to take these men to the best woodcock coverts I knew. I'd feel guilty using their time fishing. But a decision had to be made.

"I could handle a little guilt," I rationalized to myself, "in exchange for a few moments of casting a fly to a trout on the last day of the season."

Fishing with My Uncles

In five minutes I was back, in hip boots and vest, putting together my fly rod. I sneaked downstream through the brush, and tied on a number 12 Adams. I worked my way up to the rising fish and at one point seemed to have put him down with a sloppy cast. But a couple of minutes later he began to rise again. Then suddenly, "splosh!" He hit the Adams. My timing was right, and the trout was hooked. As I looked up to my companions I saw that the Trout Unlimited guy had come down the stream, and had joined the hunters on the bank.

I played the trout carefully. It had made its one thrashing leap, as freshly hooked browns often do, then surged doggedly against the current, going across, and then upstream. He then turned and went down below me before he began to tire. In a few minutes he was in my hands (I had brought no net), a male brown trout glistening in his full breeding colors: dark brown on the back, blending to yellow on the belly, bright orange spots among the black ones, dense above, thinning below. Its lower jaw was hooked upward and its teeth were strong and sharp, to intimidate a rival for a female on the spawning redds.

I briefly held the fish up to show the hunters and the fisherman, who, I learned later, had caught several trout. I often eat fish this size, but this time I unhooked it and cradled it, head upstream, for several seconds, before it suddenly surged and disappeared into the brownish water. "See you next year," I said quietly into the stream.

I must confess the trout was not 14 inches long, but 12. (He would have remained 14 if he had gotten away.)

Somehow, the woodcock hunting was more fun in the afternoon. The trout season had been properly ended. The lump was gone.

Epilogue

These stories are true, subject to the author's minor memory losses. The characters are real, most of them with their own names.

But the names of the lakes, rivers and streams, and even some of the towns have been given pseudonyms. The reason: fish, especially my favorite, the brook trout, are vulnerable to being caught by humans. It is the author's view that one should learn where and how to fish by trial and error, or from friends, preferably those who respect the forests, the wildlife, the waters and the fish that inhabit them. The discovery of fishing places in the northwoods should be cherished, respected and spared from over-fishing.

A few fish should be taken home and eaten. Thus the trout, perch, walleye or bass become part of you, and not simply something to dominate or brag about. One should savor the experience of wading a trout stream or a secluded beaver pond, and being the only person in sight when the trout are rising and taking newly hatched mayflies.

About the Author

William L. Robinson is professor emeritus of Biology at Northern Michigan University in Marquette, Michigan, where he taught for more than 30 years. He earned a Bachelor's Degree in Game Management from Michigan State College (now Michigan State University), a Master's Degree in Wildlife Biology from the University of Maine, and a Ph.D. in Zoology from the University of Toronto. He served in the U.S. Army as an alto saxophone player at Fort Knox, Kentucky, and Fort Shatter, Hawaii, from 1954 to 1956.

He is co-author of the textbook *Wildlife Ecology and Management* (Prentice Hall), author of *Fool Hen: The Spruce Grouse on the Yellow Dog Plains* (University of Wisconsin Press), and numerous articles on wildlife published in newspapers and scholarly journals.

He lives in Marquette with his springer spaniel, Millie.